Teaching Manual for

PrayerWays

Teaching Manual for

PrayerWays

by
Maryann Hakowski

Contributors
Armand Alcazar, FSC
Rev. Steven Brice
Margaret Holcombe
Carl Koch, FSC

Saint Mary's Press
Christian Brothers Publications
Winona, Minnesota

About the Author

Maryann Hakowski has more than fourteen years of experience in youth ministry and in coordinating and leading youth retreats. She has authored *Pathways to Praying with Teens* and three books of resources for youth retreats, *Vine and Branches 1, 2,* and *3,* all published by Saint Mary's Press. Currently she serves as pastoral associate at a parish in Virginia.

The publishing team for this manual included Julia Ahlers and Barbara Allaire, development editors; Cheryl Drivdahl, copy editor; Gary J. Boisvert, production editor and typesetter; Elaine Kohner, illustrator; pre-press, printing, and binding by the graphics division of Saint Mary's Press.

The acknowledgments continue on page 159.

Printed in the United States of America

Printing: 9 8 7 6 5 4 3 2 1

Year: 2003 02 01 00 99 98 97 96 95

ISBN 0-88489-259-X

"Come, let us go up to the mountain of the LORD,
        to the house of the God of Jacob;
that he may teach us his ways
        and that we may walk in his paths."

        .   .   .   .

        come, let us walk
        in the light of the LORD!

                                        (Isaiah 2:3–5)

Contents

Introduction to *PrayerWays*

Responding to a Spiritual Hunger

The challenges today's teenagers face—cultural, moral, and economic—are far more difficult than those previous generations of young people had to deal with. Being an adolescent has never been easy, but the times we now live in are particularly complex, making it harder than ever to grow safely and happily to adulthood.

The good news in the midst of the problems and pressures is that many young people today (not to mention adults) are expressing a longing for meaning and purpose in their life. They are recognizing their need for the spiritual, for a relationship with God that can help them not only to "make it" through a tough world, but, even more, to find true, lasting happiness.

PrayerWays responds to this spiritual hunger in young people by introducing them to the Catholic Christian tradition of prayer. The fundamental assumption of the course is that prayer and spirituality have *everything* to do with life. The definition of prayer given in chapter 1 of the text underlines this assumption: "Prayer is awareness of God and response to the presence of the sacred in all our life." Far from being an escape hatch, prayer is a portal for entering into our own life and the world more deeply. Thus, *PrayerWays* provides for a natural intersection of faith in God and the students' own life issues and concerns.

Course Goals and Structure

PrayerWays has these goals:
1. to introduce prayer to students as a responsive relationship with God in the context of everyday life
2. to enable students to encounter God in themselves, in others, and in creation
3. to help students develop and expand their images of God
4. to offer students experiences of various forms of Christian prayer
5. to encourage students to develop their own pattern of prayer and to grow in the spiritual life of faith, hope, and love

The first three chapters of the text serve as a basic introduction to prayer and spirituality. The next eight chapters cover various ways of praying, giving

students background on each type of prayer and practical experiences with the prayer forms. The ways of praying that are included are
- petition
- thanks and praise
- journal writing
- meditation
- praying with the Scriptures
- community prayer
- the Eucharist
- traditional prayer

Finally, the epilogue helps students reflect on the fruits of prayer in their life.

Intended primarily for eleventh and twelfth graders, this course can be used either for one semester or for part of a semester, depending on how many chapters are covered and on the extent to which activities from the text and the teaching manual are used.

You can shorten the course by selecting only some of the eight chapters that focus on the various ways of praying. Each of these chapters can be treated independently. You might also decide to concentrate only on certain sections of particular chapters. And, of course, the number of activities you choose to do in class will affect how long the course runs.

Teaching *PrayerWays*

A Spirit of Reverence

Teaching a course in prayer to young people is a unique opportunity to minister to them in ways that might not be possible in other religion courses. Although any effective religion course always puts a priority on the experience, growth, and inner life of the student, a course on prayer does this even more.

Thus, it is essential to approach this course and your students with a deep sense of reverence. As the teacher, centering yourself and tuning in to your own relationship with God can help you to see more clearly what is happening for your students. Ideally, you wil have a few minutes before each class begins to put yourself into a receptive frame of mind and heart. Being centered and prayerful will help you perceive the action of God's Spirit and follow the guidance of that Spirit during class, after class, and whenever you meet your students during the course. Being prayerful will also help you remember that everything does not depend on you and how well you teach. A loving God is in charge, working through you and the students themselves, who often minister to one another in a prayer class. A wonderful gift you can give your students is to pray for them regularly in your private prayer time—individually, by name, and as a community, in the deep awareness that you all are in God's hands.

Part of the spirit of reverence you can bring to your classes and students is to honor the different places people may be in with regard to prayer. Some are comfortable with praying aloud; others are not. Some take to writing in a journal easily and quickly; others need a long time to warm up to the idea; still others never really like it. It is important to respect the unique pace of change and development that each person seems to require.

PrayerWays as Pathways

Graphically, the text conveys on its cover and on its chapter opening pages that the various ways of praying are, in a sense, paths we take toward God and fullness of life. Prayer is seen as a moving, dynamic activity, an adventure, part of life's journey—not as a static or passive experience.

One way to explore this theme throughout the course is to ask the students to reflect on the photo that opens each chapter, considering how the road or path depicted might relate to the content of that chapter. The photos are meant to be evocative; they do not relate to their chapter in any one, absolute way. The exercise of going with the images in a class discussion and seeing where they lead can yield surprises for you and your students.

The Reflection Notebook

Because the basics of prayer need to be covered first in the course, the material on keeping a journal does not come up in the text until later—in chapter 6, "Journal Writing: A Conversation with God." However, from the beginning of the course, the students should become accustomed to writing their reflections in a notebook or journal. For that reason, in an early session of the course, you should tell your students they will need a private notebook for recording their thoughts, doing activities from the text or this teaching manual, and so on. They need not become totally familiar with how to keep a journal until you cover that topic as a class later in the course.

Whether you have access to the students' notebooks or journals is a matter for your own discretion. If students are doing assignments in them that you need to see, you will have to review them. Be sensitive to the students' possible desires to keep certain things in their journal private, though. You might want to suggest that they use a loose-leaf binder. With it, students have the option to turn in loose sheets for certain assignments and then return the pages to the binder after you have looked them over. In any case, stress to the students that whatever they give you to review will be kept confidential, unless an activity calls for students to share something they have written with another student, a small group, or the class. Frequently remind your students that sharing should never be coercive; students should discuss with others only what they are comfortable discussing. Everyone should also know that discussions of personal matters are to remain confidential within the class.

Activities

Reflection Activities in the Text

The student text has many reflection activities, which can be done by the students on their own, in pairs, in groups, as a whole class, or in some combination of these formats. These activities are signified in the text by a circular icon in the margin next to their description. Many of these activities would be appropriate for the students' journal or reflection notebook as well as for discussion.

It is not necessary to do all the activities in the text; in fact, it would probably be impossible. Pick and choose among them according to how much time you have for the course and which activities you think are most suited to your students. Students may want to do some activities from the text even if they are not assigned. They may also benefit by simply reading over a reflection activity without discussing it or writing out an answer, because doing so may stimulate them to think differently.

Activities in This Manual

For each chapter of the student text, a corresponding chapter of this teaching manual offers numerous activities beyond those given in the text. These activities are organized under the sections of the chapter to which they apply. For each section, a brief summary of what is covered in the text is followed by step-by-step descriptions of various teaching activities particular to that section.

The activities in this manual are structured for plenty of involvement and dynamic movement by students. Many of them use symbols and images rather than focusing simply on words and talk. This sometimes requires that you gather and prepare materials ahead of time. The effort that goes into doing so will be well worth it, for using these materials will give your students a more affective, attitude-changing experience. Some chapters provide complete prayer services, and the epilogue gives suggestions for a closing liturgy that incorporates activities done throughout the course.

This manual contains many more activities than could possibly be done in a semester, so you will have to decide which ones will best respond to the needs and inclinations of your students, as well as which ones you are comfortable with as a teacher.

Other Activities

If you want to develop other prayer activities beyond those in the student text and teaching manual, see appendix 1 for a list of excellent resource materials.

The Mystery of Prayer

Above all, remember that what you are doing with your students in this course is a mystery. You cannot imagine the seeds that are being planted and how they might develop and grow. *The Cloud of Unknowing*, a great medieval spiritual text by an anonymous English mystic, offers some wisdom to persons who engage in prayer. Its message is also true for those who *teach* others to pray: "The whole of [humanity] is wonderfully helped by what you are doing, in ways you do not understand."

Believe in that mystery!

CHAPTER 1

What Is Prayer?

Section A: Encountering the Sacred

Chapter 1 of the student text, specifically pages 7–11, extends an invitation to look for encounters with the sacred in our day-to-day experiences. We can glimpse the sacred in nature, through people who touch our life, and through the mystery of life and death. Also, opening the book of our own story often yields sacred moments we might otherwise take for granted.

Prayer Is . . .

This exercise gives students a chance to examine their attitudes about prayer as they begin this course.

On the first day of class, ask your students to take out a blank sheet of paper and a pen or pencil. Tell them you are going to write a sentence starter on the board and they will have 1 minute to complete the sentence. They are to write the first thing that comes to mind, be honest, and write for the entire minute.

On the board, write,
- Prayer is . . .

After a minute, request answers from the students and list their responses on the board. Checkmark answers offered by more than one person.

Wrap up the exercise with comments such as these:
- As you can see, we bring a lot of different attitudes about prayer to this course—some positive and some not so positive. Our feelings about prayer are a combination of our experiences and what we have learned thus far from our religious education.

  I encourage you to see today's descriptions of what prayer is as good starting points, and ask you to be willing to expand your understanding of prayer over our next weeks together. After all, this course is designed to help us find out what prayer is. Let's enjoy our exploration of prayer and pay attention to how our views of prayer change and grow as we go through this course.

(You may want to compare the students' views of prayer from this initial day with their views at the end of the course. If so, copy some or all of the responses on a piece of paper before erasing the board.)

Making Time for God

This activity demonstrates that we can find time in our busy life for encounters with the sacred.

Preparation

1. Gather a glass widemouthed quart jar or a glass pitcher, several colored kitchen sponges, a scissors, and a gallon jug of water. Cut up each dry sponge into ten to twelve pieces, until you have enough pieces to fill the jar or pitcher.

2. Place the *empty* jar or pitcher and the sponge pieces on a table or desk where all your students will be able to see them. Set the jug of water off to the side.

Procedure

1. Begin the activity by saying:
• We get so busy in our everyday life that sometimes it seems as though we have little or no room for God. Let me show you what I mean.

2. Ask the students to think of some of the things that fill up their life—schoolwork, sports, and so forth. Call for responses from the class, and for each response, place one of the sponge pieces in the jar or pitcher. Continue until the container is filled with sponge pieces. Then comment that although the container appears full, it actually still has plenty of room inside. Pour in water to the top of the jar or pitcher.

3. Ask the students what this demonstration taught them about making room for God in their life. Look for responses similar to the following:
• Even though our life may seem full, it always has room for God.
• God fills up the empty places in our life.
• Just as the sponges grew and became softer when water was added, God makes our life fuller and better.
• God fills our life with many good things and good people.

4. Close by encouraging your students to be open to encountering the sacred in everything they do, to letting God permeate every part of their life.

Open the Book on Your Story

This activity lets students reflect on their own story and is a good way to start the class's process of sharing in small groups. It is particularly good if many students in the class are new to one another.

Handout 1–A

Give each student a prefolded blank book cover, or give each student a piece of heavy white paper and ask the students to fold their paper into a book cover. Next, pass out a copy of handout 1–A, "Open the Book on Your Own Story," and several colored markers to each student. Instruct the students to answer the handout questions on their book cover and to be prepared to share their answers later in small groups.

Allow the students 15 to 20 minutes to answer the handout questions. Then pair off the students and invite them to share their answers with their partner. Tell them that after both partners have shared, they are to find a different partner and share again.

Variation: After the initial pairs have shared, ask each pair to join another. Now have each person tell the other pair a little about his or her partner's story.

Section B: The Christian Experience of the Sacred

Pages 12–16 of the student text highlight the Christian understanding of the sacred. Christians experience the sacred as grace, or the loving presence of God working in their life. They encounter God by entering into the paschal mystery with Jesus, and in the sacraments, which are ritual events that Christians use to worship God and express their faith. The Christian view of the sacred recognizes that all life experiences give us the opportunity to feel deeply the presence of God.

An Experience of Grace

Use the film or video *One Who Was There* to illustrate how the mystery of Jesus' death and Resurrection can greatly affect our life and our prayer.

Find out if your diocesan audiovisual library has or can obtain a copy of *One Who Was There* for you to borrow. If not, it is available for rental. See appendix 2 for details.

Show the film or video to the class. Afterward, allow a few minutes for quiet reflection. Then facilitate a large-group discussion based on the following questions:

- Why did the woman set out on her journey?
- Who are some of the people she met along the way? How did she find Jesus in these people?
- What did she remember about the life of Jesus? How did Jesus change her life?
- How did she remember Jesus' death and Resurrection?
- How did the Resurrection affect her life?
- How did reflecting on the paschal mystery help the woman find direction for her life?

🌳 From Good Friday to Easter Sunday

This written reflection exercise asks students to look at some of their losses, in light of the paschal mystery of Jesus.

Offer the following thoughts for reflection before giving your students their at-home reflection assignment:

- Butterflies are beautiful winged creatures that sail on the wind with the freedom of flight. But they were not always butterflies. They started out as caterpillars, crawling around on many legs, eating leaves, and going very short distances very slowly.

   A caterpillar never gets to be a butterfly unless it stops being a caterpillar. It must give up its former life on the ground, enter a cocoon, and wait to transform into a being with a new life in the air.

   The student text says, "New life can come out of loss," and presents the story about Connie to illustrate that idea. Everyone suffers small losses and large losses. These losses are never easy. And when you are in the midst of suffering one, it is difficult to imagine that something life-giving can come out of it.

   When Jesus' disciples were watching him die on the cross, they never imagined how glorious his Resurrection would be. The mystery of Jesus' death and Resurrection is that there will always be an Easter Sunday after a Good Friday.

Instruct the students to take a few minutes at home to reflect on some of the losses they have suffered, in light of the paschal mystery. Tell them to record their thoughts in their reflection notebook. Encourage them to think about how the losses transformed them in some way. Urge them to ask Jesus for some special help if they are in the midst of dealing with a particularly tough loss right now.

(See page 11 of this teaching manual for more information about the use of reflection notebooks for this course.)

🌳 Signs of the Sacred

This out-of-class assignment helps students learn about how sacraments can be encounters with the sacred.

Ask your students to interview someone who has recently celebrated a sacrament or helped someone else celebrate a sacrament. The focus of the interview should be on how the experience was an encounter with the sacred and on how the experience transformed the person's life. Tell the students to summarize their interview in a two-page essay.

Offer the students these or other suggestions for people to interview:

- a confirmation sponsor
- a godparent at an infant baptism
- a new bride or groom
- a recently ordained priest
- an adult who has completed a Rite of Christian Initiation of Adults (RCIA) program at her or his parish
- the teacher of a First Communion class
- a recipient of the sacrament of anointing
- a retired parish priest

Section C: Responding to the Sacred

This section of the chapter, pages 16–17 in the student text, discusses several ways we can respond to the sacred in our life. Some people try to explain away sacred experiences or make fun of them. Others welcome the experiences and respond to them with faith and courage, trusting in God's presence.

Through the Eyes of Faith

This activity demonstrates how everything changes when seen through the eyes of faith.

Have several pairs of 3-D glasses on hand and introduce the activity with comments such as these:

- People who wear prescription glasses or contact lenses know how dramatically the world changes when they put them on. A similar thing happens when we put on sunglasses on a bright, sunny day. Donning the eyes of faith is a little like putting on prescription glasses or contact lenses or sunglasses—it changes the way we see the world. Actually, it's more like putting on 3-D glasses—it lets us see the world in depth.

Pass the 3-D glasses around the room so that everyone can look through them.

Handout 1–B

At this point, distribute handout 1–B, "Through the Eyes of Faith." Tell the students that this handout is meant to help them see ways their life can look different through the eyes of faith. Give the students 15 minutes or so to complete the handout.

Split the class into groups of three, and invite the students to share their responses to the handout within their small group.

Variation: If 3-D glasses are not available, explain that when we look at the world without the eyes of faith, it is as if we are a nearsighted person without prescription glasses or contact lenses. Our view of the world is not as full, bright, and clear as it could be. Then proceed with handout 1–B and the small-group discussion.

Section D: How Does Prayer Fit In?

Pages 17–19 in the student text introduce the basic definition of prayer used in the course: "Prayer is awareness of God and response to the presence of the sacred in all our life." In other words, prayer is more than words and thoughts; it takes shape in our day-to-day life.

Living Prayers

This in-class reflection and discussion lets students explore, in concrete terms, the definition of prayer given on page 17 of their text.

Review with your students the definition of prayer given in their text. Explain that according to this definition, each of us has the opportunity to live prayerfully, to be aware of God's presence and to let that presence affect how we live and how we treat others.

Then ask the students to spend 10 minutes responding to the following questions in their reflection notebook:
- How has an awareness of God changed my life?
- How has an awareness of God affected how I treat other people?
- What can I do to make every day a living prayer?

Pair off the students and invite them to share their responses with their partner.

Top Ten Reasons to Pray

This activity is a fun exercise to help students brainstorm ways that prayer can make a difference.

Form small groups of four or five students and instruct them to brainstorm their top ten reasons to pray. Tell the groups to record their reasons, and encourage them to be creative and positive.

Ask a spokesperson from each group to read the group's list to the rest of the class. Collect the lists and post them on a classroom bulletin board.

Open the Book on Your Own Story

Answer the following questions in marker on the outside of your blank book cover. Make your cover look like a real book jacket: put your title, the answer to question 1, on the front; put the answers for questions 2 to 8, in complete sentences, on the back or on the inside flaps.

1. If you were to write a book about your life, what would be the title?

2. Where does your story begin?

3. Who are the most important characters in your book?

4. What are some of the settings for your story?

5. What is one high point in your story?

6. What is one low point in your story?

7. Where does God fit into your story?

8. What do you expect to happen to you next?

Through the Eyes of Faith

Complete the following sentences in the spaces provided:

1. If I put on the eyes of faith, **my family** would look . . .

2. If I put on the eyes of faith, **tough decisions** would look . . .

3. If I put on the eyes of faith, **my friends** would look . . .

4. If I put on the eyes of faith, **my schoolwork** would look . . .

5. If I put on the eyes of faith, **my problems** would look . . .

6. If I put on the eyes of faith, **my prayer life** would look . . .

7. If I put on the eyes of faith, **my future** would look . . .

CHAPTER 2

Where Do We Meet God?

Section A: Encountering God in Self

Pages 21–27 of the student text explain that to answer the question Where do we meet God? we must begin with ourselves. God created human beings as images of God. So, at the deepest part of every human self, God is present. Encountering God's presence within us requires that we come to know ourselves as truly and fully as possible.

Creating Commercials

This group activity helps raise students' awareness of the sharp contrast between the effect of advertising on self-esteem and self-knowledge and the effect of seeing oneself as created in God's image.

Begin with a statement along these lines:

- Let's take a critical look at the way advertising affects our culture and our view of ourselves. We will do that by turning the tables on the types of messages we encounter through the media. Instead of seeing ourselves through the eyes of the media, we will be looking at ourselves through the eyes of God. As we will see, very different messages come through when we do this.

Break the class into groups of six to eight students. Ask each group to prepare a 1- to 2-minute TV commercial that encourages people to be themselves, to discover and celebrate their unique gifts. Convey the following guidelines and give the groups 10 to 15 minutes to prepare their commercial:

- Each group may do a parody of an existing commercial or create an entirely new commercial.
- Each person in a group should have a role in planning and presenting the commercial to the class.
- The groups should use humor and creativity and readily available props.

After all the commercials have been presented, lead a brief discussion. Elicit responses to these two questions:

- How do the messages of your commercials differ from the ones you regularly encounter in the media?
- How might commercials that reflect God's view of people affect their self-esteem and self-knowledge?

Close by encouraging the students to become more aware of the messages they receive from the media. Say something to this effect:

- The next time you see a commercial on TV or an ad in a magazine, ask yourself these two questions: (1) Does the ad's message decrease or increase my self-esteem and self-knowledge? (2) Does the message of the ad support or oppose God's view of me?

Variation: Instead of using drama, ask each group to create a visual advertisement that encourages people to be themselves. Supply each group with poster board, old magazines, markers, scissors, tape, and glue. Ask each group to select a spokesperson to present its ad to the entire class. Follow the presentations with the discussion questions and wrap-up comments given for the main activity.

Behind the Picket Fence

This activity picks up on the discussion "Hiding from Our Real Self" in the student text, page 25. It encourages students to get in touch with their true self and to share that self with others.

1. Several days before doing this activity with the class, ask a couple of students to draw a large picket fence on a piece of butcher paper as long as the front wall of the classroom. The pickets and the spaces between them should be of equal width and about as tall as the paper is wide. Tape the fence to the wall at the beginning of the class period in which it will be used.

2. Initiate the discussion with a quick review of the material under "Hiding from Our Real Self" in the student text. Note the difference between our true self—the one we show only to people we trust—and the self we usually want other people to see.

3. Give the students a few minutes to jot down qualities they think most young people want others to see in them. Offer an example, as in, "Most young people want others to see them as tough or as independent." The students could also think of qualities they think others want to see in young people, such as obedience or politeness. Ask each student to share one idea. With a marker, write the qualities on the pickets of the butcher-paper fence. Then, briefly discuss these questions:
   - Why do young people want to appear this way to others?
   - Why do others want young people to appear this way?

4. Ask the students to jot down some of the qualities they think most young people are likely to hide from others. For example, you might say, "Most young people are likely to hide their spirituality from others." After a few minutes, ask each student to share an idea, and write the qualities they mention, in marker, in the spaces between the pickets. Follow up with these discussion questions:
   - What keeps us from showing our true self?
   - Why is it important to let our true self shine through the fences we have put up?

Variation 1: To help the students discover what qualities they project as their outward appearance and what qualities reflect their true self, use handout 2–A, "Behind the Picket Fence."

Begin with step 2 from the main activity. Then instruct the students to fill out handout 2–A individually, and give them about 5 minutes do so. Next, divide the class into groups of two or three and give the students 5 to 10 minutes to share with one another what they wrote on their handout. Wrap up with a large-group discussion on the questions posed in step 4 of the main activity.

Variation 2: Begin with step 2 from the main activity. Then ask the students to complete handout 2–A individually, either in class or at home.

A Kaleidoscope Prayer Service

A prayer service setting such as the one detailed here can be a powerful and effective way to invite students to let their true self shine through.

Preparation

Handout 2–B

1. Several days before the prayer service, recruit two or three students to make a large poster with a colored kaleidoscope image on it. Give them handout 2–B, "A Sample Kaleidoscope Image," to use as a model, along with poster board and any other needed art materials. Ensure that the completed image has a separate space for each person in your class.

Handout 2–C

2. Select six students to do the readings on handout 2–C, "Voices for 'A Kaleidoscope Prayer Service.'" Distribute a copy of handout 2–C to each reader and assign her or him a voice number. Practice this part of the service with the students beforehand so that they know when to read their parts.

3. Purchase several small kaleidoscopes, a minimum of one for each ten students. Obtain a tape or CD of Cyndi Lauper's song "True Colors" (available on *True Colors,* Portrait tape cassette or compact disk 40313, October 1986).

4. Determine where the service is to be held, and reserve the space if necessary. You will need enough room for the entire class to gather in a circle.

5. Along with the poster, the kaleidoscopes, and the "True Colors" tape or CD, gather these supplies: several large black markers, a tape player or CD player, an extension cord (if needed), masking tape or an easel, and a piece of cloth (such as a small blanket or large scarf) or a small box.

6. On the day of the service, hide the kaleidoscopes under the cloth or box in the center of the space you will be using for the prayer service. Set up the tape player or CD player and make sure the tape or CD is set at the beginning of the song "True Colors." Display the kaleidoscope poster, either taped on the wall or set on the easel, and place the markers nearby.

Procedure

1. Begin the service by gathering the students into a circle. Call them to prayer with words such as these, speaking slowly and clearly:

- In our studies, we have learned that knowing our true self is the beginning point of fully encountering God in prayer. In discovering the colorful kaleidoscope that is our true self, we open ourselves to countless possibilities for meeting God in prayer.

2. Continue by saying something like the following:

- Sadly, however, we try to keep our true self—our true colors—hidden most of the time.

At this point, the six readers say their "Hidden Colors" parts in turn—first voice 1, then voice 2, and so on. As each reader says their part, they turn away with their back to the inside of the circle.

3. Pause a moment or two after voice 6 has turned away, and then continue to guide the prayer service with remarks along these lines:

- We may choose to hide our true self for many reasons. Perhaps we think that what's really there is ugly, not good enough, or not lovable. But the God whom we seek to encounter in prayer, and who abides in us, loves us the way we are. This God calls each of us to let our true self shine through—to love our self as wholly as God does. The more we learn to love ourselves, the richer and fuller our relationships will be— with ourselves, with God, and with others.

Now, in turn, the six voices say their "True Colors" parts, turning to face the inside of the circle as they do so.

4. Remove the piece of cloth or the box to uncover the kaleidoscopes, and distribute them to the students. Begin a period of reflection with a comment such as this:

- Let's take a few moments to reflect on how we are each like a kaleidoscope—ever changing and ever beautiful.

Instruct the students to look reflectively through the kaleidoscope for a few seconds and then to pass the kaleidoscope to the person to their left. Make sure everyone has looked through a kaleidoscope before proceeding. Continue the reflection with words similar to these:

- The pattern of the kaleidoscope can be seen only if we look through it; the patterns change only if we turn the kaleidoscope. God of all life and love, help us to look inside unafraid and to see the beauty in ourselves. Grant us the courage to let our true colors shine through in all we do.

5. Conclude the prayer service by playing the song "True Colors." As the song plays, invite the students to come forward one at a time to sign their name on one of the spaces of the kaleidoscope poster, as a symbol of their promise to try to let their true colors shine through. You may sign the poster too.

Variation 1: Ask six students to write scripts for the "Hidden Colors" and "True Colors" voices based on their own experiences.

Variation 2: Although designed to be used with the section "Encountering God in Self" in the student text, this prayer service could also serve as a wrap-up for the whole chapter. To adapt the activity for this use, you may want to reword the speaking parts for the teacher to make them include more of the major themes of the entire chapter.

Section B: Encountering God in Others

This section of the chapter, pages 28–31 in the student text, focuses on how we meet God in others. For Christians, this way of encountering God centers around membership in the Body of Christ.

We Are Members of Christ's Body

This reflection may be used as a quiet way to open or close the class period in which students begin the section "Encountering God in Others."

First, ask for quiet and state that you would like the class to reflect on the role young people play as members of Christ's Body, the church. Tell them you will be reading to them a passage from Saint Paul's First Letter to the Corinthians. Ask the students to listen carefully as you read, and to recognize that they are the eyes, ears, hands, and feet of Christ. Then, slowly and clearly, read 1 Cor. 12:12–27.

After you have finished reading the passage, ask the class to spend a few minutes writing reflectively about one gift they bring to the Body of Christ or one thing they do to help build up the Body of Christ.

Close by playing the song "We Are One Body," the theme of Pope John Paul II's World Youth Day in Denver in 1993. It is on the tape or CD *Say Yes*, by Dana, published by Heartbeat Records in 1993 (see appendix 2 for details).

Variation: For a more animated reflection on how young people participate in the Body of Christ, you will need a ball of white string or yarn, masking tape, and scissors.

Arrange the room so that the students sit facing one another in a large circle. In the middle of the circle, using the string or yarn, create an outline of a person lying on the floor. Use the tape to hold the string or yarn in place.

Ask the students to think of ways they build up the Body of Christ, while they listen to your reading of the passage from First Corinthians. After the reading, call the students to the center of the circle one by one, to share one of their ideas. Tell the students to stand near the body part of the string or yarn figure that best describes the way they build up the Body of Christ. Demonstrate what they are to do. Go stand near the feet and say,

- For example, you could stand by the feet and say, "I am like the feet because I go wherever I am needed to help others out."

Assure the students that it is okay to choose a part of the body that others have already spoken about. Continue until each person has had a chance to share a reflection. Close the activity with the Lord's Prayer.

Finding God in Others

Handout 2–D

This written reflection will help students understand that God is revealed to us most often through other people.

Pass out handout 2–D, "Finding God in Others." Ask the students to take the handout home, find a quiet place to read the story, and then reflect on what they have read for a few minutes. After this, they are to spend some time

2

writing about ways they can find God in their classmates, family members, and other people.

Variation: Follow up the written reflection with an in-class discussion or sharing session.

Searching for God in Others

Cameras and photographs often afford us the opportunity to see things that, in our normal routine, we can easily miss. This activity engages students in a photographic search to recognize God in others.

Send the students off to look for photos in family albums or to take new photos. Suggest alternatives to students who want to take new photos but do not have a camera: sharing, borrowing, and purchasing a disposable camera like the Kodak Fun Saver are possibilities. Tell the students to look for photos of people who reflect God or Jesus through word or action. You will probably want to give the students from several days to a week to conduct their search.

Ask the students each to bring at least two photos to class. Give them about 10 minutes to share their photos with one another in small groups of four or five.

Wrap up the activity with a large-group discussion. Begin with questions such as these:

- Did you find it difficult or easy to find people who reflect God or Jesus?
- Will doing this search affect the way you look at your friends and family members? strangers?
- How might this search for God in others affect your understanding of yourself?

Variation: Ask each student to contribute a photo of someone who reflects God or Jesus through word or action, and a caption for it. Create a photo gallery and display it in the classroom to remind the students that God is present all around them.

Section C: Encountering God in Creation

Pages 32–34 of the student text explain that just as we cannot help but encounter the artist when we view a work of art, we meet God in all that God has created. The Christian Scriptures are filled with examples of encountering God in creation.

God in Creation

This activity illustrates how nature can serve as a springboard for communication with God.

Ask the students to recall a time when they encountered God in creation or felt close to God in the outdoors.

Ask them to close their eyes and journey to that time or place in their mind, remembering the sights, sounds, smells, and textures in detail, as well as how they felt. Pause for a moment or two, and then ask them to consider this question:

- How was God trying to speak to you?

After a few minutes of silent reflection, tell the students to slowly open their eyes and come back to full awareness. Conclude by stressing the importance of taking time to be alone with God and of being open to encountering God in nature.

Variation 1: Ask the students to write a thank-you letter to God for a time when they encountered God in creation.

Variation 2: Encourage the students to find some time in the next week to spend alone with God.

Jesus and Nature in the Christian Testament

This activity shows students that Jesus often used nature examples to teach about himself and God.

To do this activity, each student should have a copy of the Christian Testament. Also, although biblical concordances are not necessary, if some are available you may want to have them on hand for the class to use.

Divide the class into groups of three to four students. Instruct the groups to search through the four Gospels to find passages in which Jesus used nature to reveal something about himself or to teach something about God.

Offer the class some examples:

- John 15:1–8 (Jesus is the vine, we are the branches.)
- Matthew 13:31–32 (The Reign of God is like a mustard seed.)

If you are using concordances, pass them out to the groups. These may be shared among the groups if you do not have enough for each group to have its own. You may need to give some brief instructions on how to use a concordance.

Instruct each group to come up with at least five examples and to discuss what the passages teach about God or Jesus.

Variation 1: After the main activity, conduct a large-group discussion in which each small group shares with the class one passage it found and what the group learned from it.

Variation 2: Ask the groups to record their passages as they locate them. After the groups finish their discussion, collect their lists. Compile the passages on these lists into a handout to be distributed to the students for their own reference and reflection.

Creation Praise: Psalm 148

Handout 2–E

2

This prayerful reading of Psalm 148 helps students see how the marvelous gifts of creation provide us with many opportunities to encounter God.

Distribute handout 2–E, "Creation Praise: Psalm 148." Designate a right and a left side of the classroom. Instruct the students to pray the psalm out loud in an alternating fashion, following the cues on the handout.

Give the students about 5 minutes to jot down ways the psalm illustrates how God is present in creation. They can do their writing on the back of their handout.

Take a few minutes to let the students share some of their responses. Close by encouraging the students to look for God's presence in the world around them on a regular basis.

Behind the Picket Fence

1. On the pickets of the fence, write down the qualities you let others see about yourself, or the qualities you would like others to see.

2. On the spaces between the pickets, write down the qualities about yourself that you tend to hide from others.

A Sample Kaleidoscope Image

Use this image as a model to make the kaleidoscope poster for the kaleido-scope prayer service.

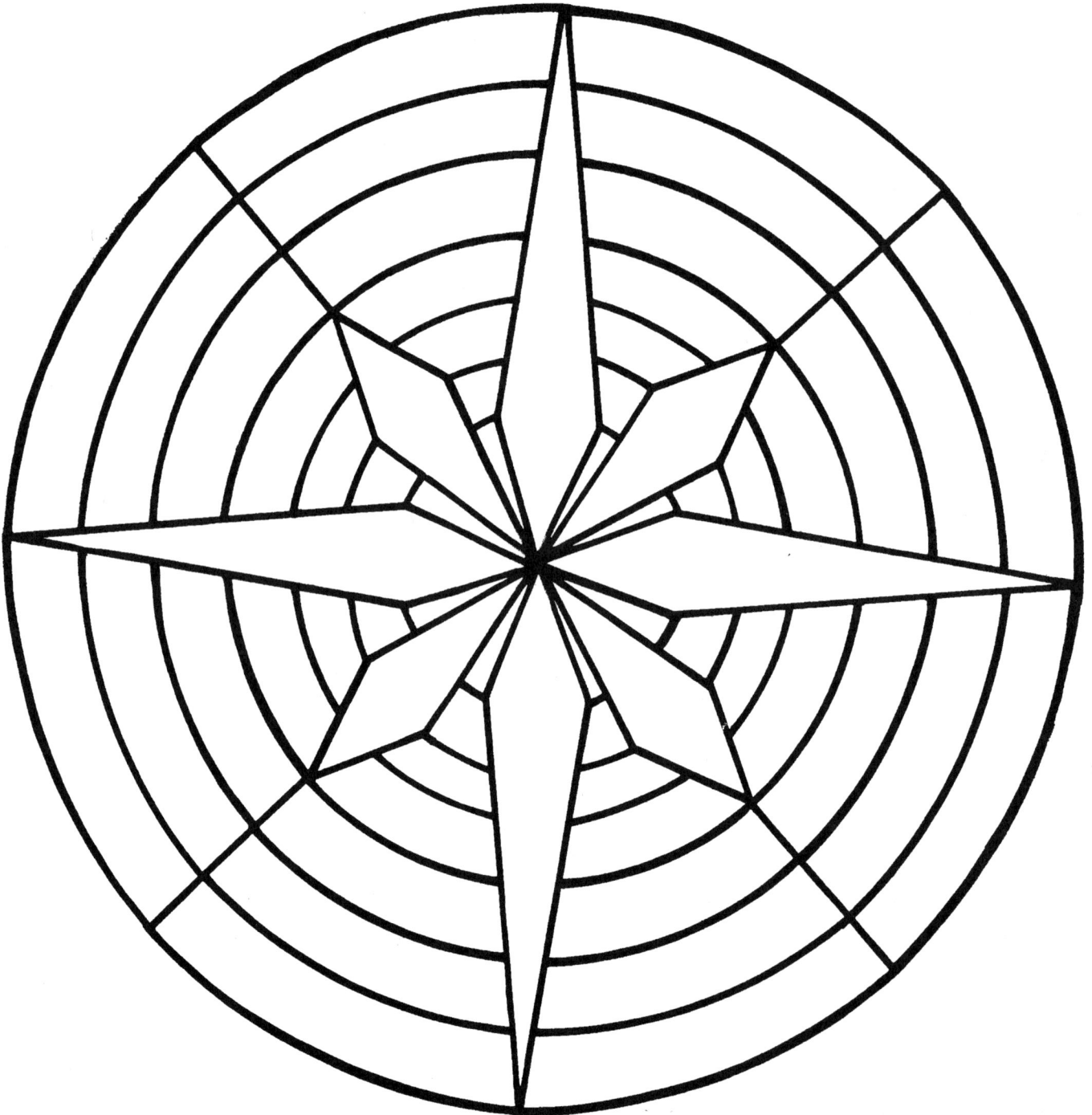

Voices for "A Kaleidoscope Prayer Service"

Hidden Colors

Voice 1: I can't talk to my parents anymore; no one has time to listen to me.

Voice 2: I am doing worse and worse in chemistry class. I just know I am going to flunk my next test.

Voice 3: I want to ask Sharon to the dance, but I am afraid she will turn me down.

Voice 4: I really want to play on the basketball team. What will I do if I don't make the first cut?

Voice 5: My parents are always bugging me to go to church on Sunday, but what if my friends see me there?

Voice 6: I don't want to go to that party—I know people will be drinking there. But I don't want to sit home alone.

True Colors

Voice 1: Mom, can we talk? It's really important. Can you make some time for me?

Voice 2: Ms. Brown, I'm really struggling with chemistry, but I'd like to do better. Would you help me find a tutor?

Voice 3: Sharon, would you like to go to the dance with me? We could stop for some pizza afterward.

Voice 4: I think I'll play some basketball at the Y; I'll practice every day so I'll be ready for the tryouts.

Voice 5: John, why don't we go together to the youth group Mass this Sunday. Maybe we will meet some new people there.

Voice 6: Sue, are you worried about what might happen at this party, too? Why don't we go see a movie instead?

Handout 2–C: Permission to reproduce this handout for classroom use is granted.

31

Finding God in Others

Attentively read this story. Then take a few moments to reflect quietly on its meaning. On the back of this handout, write about some ways you can find the Lord in your classmates and family, and in the world around you.

Where Are You, Lord?

The parish priest in a town named Austerity climbed way up in the church's steeple to be nearer to God. He wanted to hand down God's Word to his parishioners, like Moses of old. Then, one day he indeed thought he heard God say something.

The priest cried aloud from the steeple, "Where are you, Lord? I can't seem to hear your voice clearly."

And the Lord replied, "I'm down here among my people. Where are you?"

(Brewer Mattocks, from Brian Cavanaugh, *More Sower's Seeds*, pages 8–9)

Handout 2–D: Permission to reproduce this handout for classroom use is granted.

Creation Praise: Psalm 148

All: Praise the LORD!

Right: Praise the LORD from the heavens;
praise him in the heights!

Left: Praise him, all his angels;
praise him, all his host!

Right: Praise him, sun and moon;
praise him, all you shining stars!

Left: Praise him, you highest heavens,
and you waters above the heavens!

Right: Let them praise the name of the LORD,
for he commanded and they were created.

Left: He established them forever and ever;
he fixed their bounds, which cannot be passed.

Right: Praise the LORD from the earth,
you sea monsters and all deeps,

Left: fire and hail, snow and frost,
stormy wind fulfilling his command!

Right: Mountains and all hills,
fruit trees and all cedars!

Left: Wild animals and all cattle,
creeping things and flying birds!

Right: Kings of the earth and all peoples,
princes and all rulers of the earth!

Left: Young men and women alike,
old and young together!

Right: Let them praise the name of the LORD,
for his name alone is exalted;
his glory is above earth and heaven.

Left: He has raised up a horn for his people,
praise for all his faithful,
for the people of Israel who are close to him.

All: Praise the LORD!

(Psalm 148)

On the back of this handout, jot down ways the psalm
illustrates how God is present in creation.

CHAPTER 3

Who Is the God We Encounter in Prayer?

3

Section A: Metaphors and Images

The introductory section of this chapter, pages 35–38 in the student text, addresses the role of metaphors and images in prayer, especially how our images of God influence our prayer experience. Because no one human image can fully describe God, many images are needed. The Trinity—God as Father, Son, and Spirit—provides the core images for the Christian understanding of God.

Images of God

This reflection helps students recognize that their images of God influence how they pray. Use this activity before your students read the introductory section of the chapter in the student text.

Give each student a blank index card and a colored marker or crayon. Proceed with these instructions:

- I am going to say a word. Write down or draw the first image that comes to mind when you hear that word. Do not take a long time to think about your response.

    The word is *God*.

After 2 to 3 minutes, break the class into small groups of three or four students and invite the students to share their image and why they chose it.

Conclude this reflection activity with a brief preview of the main themes of the chapter as they are given in the student text:

- We commonly use metaphors and images to describe our experiences of God.
- The images we hold of God influence our prayer.
- We need many images to describe God.
- The Trinity is the main image Christians use for understanding God.

Then assign "Metaphors and Images" in the student text, pages 35–38, for reading. Encourage the students to be open to exploring the images of God discussed in the chapter.

A note on the Trinity: Although the dogma of the Trinity is introduced in this first section of the chapter, no activities related to it are offered at this point. Instead, it is recommended that activities meant to help students experience the Trinity as an image for prayer be used to wrap up the class's work with chapter 3. The suggested Trinity activities are "Praise Cards" and "Three-in-One Prayer Experience," on pages 39–40 in this manual.

Section B:
Enhancing Our Images of God the Father

Pages 38–42 of the student text highlight some of the main scriptural images in the Christian tradition for God as the First Person of the Trinity. Students are invited to explore the richness of these images and to include them in their prayer experience.

Who Is Your God?

Handout 3–A

This exercise uses statements describing God to help students assess and expand their view of God.

Give each student a copy of handout 3–A, "Who Is Your God?" Tell the students to follow the directions and fill out the handout on their own.

Pair off the students. Then invite the partners to share three images they agree with and three they disagree with.

Conclude by pointing out the necessity and value of holding more than one image of God.

Variation: Assign handout 3–A for home reflection. Instruct the students to compose a personal prayer in their reflection notebook, using their favorite image of God.

Images of God Come Alive

This activity asks students to write short stories as a means to experience in a tangible way the scriptural images of God discussed in their text.

1. Introduce this activity by reiterating the point made on page 36 of the student text, that our images of God are necessarily based on our own experience, understanding, and imagination. Note that even many of the images of God relayed in the Scriptures emerge from or are based on people's experience of God. In addition, it is only through our everyday experiences that the images come alive and have meaning for us today.

2. Divide the class into six groups. Assign one of the following images to each group:
- God sets the people free ("I AM").
- Anything is possible with God (all-powerful God).
- God is light in our darkness (God as light and guide).
- Our Mother in heaven comforts us (feminine images of God).
- We are the sheep of God's flock (God as shepherd).
- Daddy is always there for us (God as *Abba*).

Tell the groups to write a brief story about how someone today might experience God as described in their assigned image. Their story can be fictional or based on a true-life situation; it can also be a modern adaptation of a biblical story. Give the groups about 20 minutes to write their story.

3. Invite the groups to share their story with the rest of the class. Allow a few minutes for discussion after each story.

Variation: Use this activity for a home assignment. Assign one image of God to each student, and tell the students to write a short story on their own. In class the next day, have the students share their stories in small groups.

Section C: Exploring Our Images of God the Son

On pages 43–46, the student text explores some of the main scriptural images associated with Jesus as God's Son, the Second Person of the Trinity. As they read their text, students are encouraged to reflect on the role these images, and the many other images of Jesus found in the Scriptures, might have on their prayer.

Who Is Jesus?

This activity invites students to brainstorm some of the many names and images connected with Jesus with which they are already familiar. Do this activity before assigning the reading of the section "Exploring Our Images of God the Son" in the student text.

1. Direct your students to take out a blank sheet of paper and a pen or pencil. Give them 5 minutes to list as many names and images of Jesus as they can. They can draw from experience, the Scriptures, family traditions, and so forth.

2. Call for a name or image of Jesus from the class, and write it on a large piece of poster board hung where all can see it. Continue to ask for names of Jesus until all the students' responses are listed on the poster.

3. Close by affirming the students' awareness of images of Jesus. Also affirm the value of having many images of Jesus to call upon in prayer—that it expands the ways we can relate to and experience Jesus. Invite the students to be open to the images of Jesus discussed in their text, if these are unfamiliar, and to incorporating images of Jesus in their own prayer.

Variation: Leave the poster up throughout the time you work on this section, and allow the students to add names or images to the poster as they work with the text material on Jesus.

Meeting Jesus in the Scriptures

This Scripture search lets students discover some of the rich, descriptive images of Jesus found in the Scriptures.

Handout 3–B

Distribute handout 3–B, "Images of Jesus in the Scriptures," to your students and instruct them to follow the directions given on the handout. Assign the handout to be done in class or as homework.

3

Answers to handout questions: When all the students have completed their handout, read the answers as follows:
1. Lamb of God
2. Servant
3. King of Kings
4. Prince of Peace
5. Lord and Messiah
6. Shepherd
7. Resurrection and Life
8. Prophet
9. Teacher
10. Brother
11. Bread
12. Hope
13. Healer

Variation: After the students finish the Scripture search, direct them to choose the image they are *least* comfortable or familiar with and to write about how this image opens up a new aspect to their relationship with Jesus. Tell them to record their thoughts in their reflection notebook.

Section D: Praying with the Holy Spirit

This section, pages 46–50 in the student text, focuses on images of the Holy Spirit, or the love between the Father and the Son. The images examined help show how the Spirit acts in our life, in our heart, and in our prayer.

Calling on the Holy Spirit

This prayer-writing exercise invites students to discover how the Spirit can help them in their everyday life.

1. Assign the section "Praying with the Holy Spirit" in the student text, pages 46–50, as homework before using this activity.

2. After the students have done the reading, review the key points of the section in class, especially the material on Pentecost. Stress that the Spirit is an active, dynamic force in our daily life, rather than a passive gift we receive only on confirmation day.

Explain that in traditional Christian terms, the Spirit is active in our life through the seven gifts of the Holy Spirit. List these gifts on the board:

- wisdom
- knowledge
- understanding
- courage
- right judgment
- reverence
- wonder and awe

3. Ask your students to take out their reflection notebook. Instruct them to think about each of the seven gifts of the Holy Spirit and then, for each gift, write a brief prayer asking the Spirit to help them deal with specific challenges in their life. Give the students 15 minutes to write their prayers. Offer an example to get them started:

- Spirit, please give me the courage to go against the crowd sometimes and be my own person.

4. Wrap up the activity in a prayerful manner. Lead with the following words, and then ask each student to share aloud with the class one of his or her prayers:

- Spirit of God, our helper, intercessor, counselor, and protector, we bring these prayers before you in trust and in hope.

Once everyone has offered their prayer, conclude by praying:

- Gracious Spirit, we thank you for hearing our prayers. Dwell within our hearts and our minds now and always. Amen.

Variation: Instead of concluding this activity with a prayer-sharing time, you may want your students to reserve these prayers for part C of the "Three-in-One Prayer Experience" outlined on pages 39–40 of this manual.

The Spirit Working in My Life

This written reflection urges students to become more aware of the power of the Spirit working in their everyday life.

1. Begin by reiterating the point that the Spirit is always with us, that this was Jesus' promise to us before he ascended into heaven. Sometimes, however, we forget this and go about our daily life unaware of how the Spirit touches us and works through us to touch others. Relate some examples, such as these:

- On a whim, you call a friend just when she or he really needs a kind ear.
- You get an extra boost of energy to help you do well in a track meet.
- On the radio, you hear words in a song that really match what you are going through right now.

2. Tell your students that for the next week, they have the opportunity to rekindle their awareness of the Spirit in their life. Instruct them to write in their reflection notebook at least one entry a day on how the Spirit has touched them or worked through them to touch others. Let the students know that they can do this reflection at the end of the day or at any time they feel inspired to write something down.

✿ Praise Cards

This activity helps students write and share prayer cards of praise and thanksgiving addressed to all three persons of the Trinity.

Pass out handout 3–C, "Praise Cards," and assign it for in-class work or as homework. Advise your students to pause and think about the many ways God, Jesus, and the Holy Spirit have blessed them, before they fill out the handout. Suggest that they jot down on scrap paper or in their reflection notebook any ideas or thoughts that come to mind during this reflection. Then, when they have considered all three persons of the Trinity, they should be ready to compose prayers of praise and thanksgiving for these many blessings.

The students may trade praise cards with one another and use them in their own prayer or reflection writing at home.

✿ Three-in-One Prayer Experience

This activity provides a general framework for students to use to create a prayer service that ties together the main themes of the chapter. Use it to conclude the class's work on metaphors and images of God in prayer.

Preparation

1. A day or so before holding the prayer service, divide the class into three groups and assign one of the following prayer service parts to each group: part A—God the Father; part B—God the Son; and part C—God the Holy Spirit.

2. Pass on the following instructions to the class:
- Each group is responsible for preparing one part of the prayer service we will use to conclude our work with this chapter. Each part should include three components:
  —*A scriptural reading:* The passage chosen should express some aspect of your group's assigned person of the Trinity and should be proclaimed by a reader or group of readers. You may use a biblical concordance to help you find the passage you like.
  —*A contemporary song:* You may play all or part of a song that shares a message about your assigned person of the Trinity. The song may open your part of the service, follow your scriptural passage, or be used at whatever point you decide.
  —*A prayer to share:* This prayer should be original and should reflect your experiences as young people with the person of the Trinity you are assigned. Consider writing and sharing prayers of petition, or a prayer of praise. The prayer may be read by one or all of the members of your group.
- Remember, all three components must be included in your part of the prayer service, but you may arrange the components in any order you choose. The order of the parts of the service will correspond with the order of the Trinity, unless someone comes up with a more creative idea.

3. Allow the groups class time to prepare their part of the service. Provide biblical concordances or direct the groups to the library or media center for these resources. Arrange for the use of a tape player or CD player.

Procedure

On the day of the prayer service, gather as a class in a meeting space different from your regular classroom, such as the school chapel or library. Proceed with the prayer service as planned by the students. Afterward, affirm and thank the students for their efforts.

3

Who Is Your God?

Here are some statements people use to describe God. Some may be familiar, others not. Place a check mark before the ones you agree with; place an *X* before the ones you disagree with.

___ the only person who loves me for myself

___ the computer that programs the universe

___ a puppeteer who manipulates people like toys

___ an energy people discover when a baby is born or they fall in love

___ an unseen universal soul people are a part of

___ a creator who believes that everything created is good

___ a force that was active during biblical times but not today

___ a father who loves his children selflessly

___ a mother who nurtures her children

___ someone who forgives all my mistakes

___ a being beyond my words or understanding

___ an eccentric being who created the world and forgot about it

___ someone who dares to let me be free

___ a being who gave me life

___ a lawgiver who commands me to do right, not wrong

___ a ruler whose power is freedom and love, rather than force

___ a lover who invites me to a heavenly marriage feast

___ an idea created by past generations to explain the world

___ the peace bringer who will reign when people are as sisters and brothers

___ the perfect one who makes me feel guilty

___ the one who wants me to become myself

___ a cosmic clown who created joy and laughter

___ other (specify) _____

___ other (specify) _____

Images of Jesus in the Scriptures

Read the following passages and identify the image of Jesus used in each:

1. John 1:29 _____
2. Luke 22:27 _____
3. Revelation 19:16 _____
4. Isaiah 9:6 _____
5. Acts 2:36 _____
6. 1 Peter 5:4 _____
7. John 11:25 _____
8. Luke 4:24 _____
9. Mark 4:1–2 _____
10. Hebrews 2:11 _____
11. John 6:51 _____
12. 1 Timothy 1:1 _____
13. Matthew 8:2–3 _____

Praise Cards

Spend some time reflecting about the many ways God, Jesus, and the Holy Spirit have blessed you. Then, using the forms provided here, compose prayers of praise and thanksgiving for these many blessings.

O Jesus,

I praise and thank you for

_____

_____

_____

_____

_____

_____

_____

O Spirit,

I praise and thank you for

_____

_____

_____

_____

_____

_____

O God,

I praise and thank you for

_____

_____

_____

_____

_____

_____

CHAPTER 4

Petition: Asking God for Help

Section A: "Please, God . . ."

The opening section of this chapter in the student text, pages 51–52, introduces one of the most familiar ways Christians pray: prayers of petition, or prayers asking God for help. Prayers of petition flow out of a trust that God cares about us and wants to hear from us. Although we should not limit our prayer to this form alone, prayers of petition offer us a direct way to bring our everyday concerns and needs to God's loving attention.

Ask. Seek. Knock.

This prayer service gives students an opportunity to bring their prayers of petition to God. It builds upon the invitation Jesus offers in Matt. 7:7–11, that is, to ask, to seek, and to knock. The service may be used to begin or conclude the class's work with prayers of petition.

Preparation

1. Gather the following materials:
- long, multicolored pipe cleaners, one for each student
- two Bibles

Handout 4–A
- three copies of handout 4–A, "Knock . . ."
- a wooden object that can easily be held in one hand and is suitable for knocking on, such as a cutting board
- songbooks containing the song "Seek Ye First," by Karen Lafferty, preferably one for each student ("Seek Ye First" can be found in most contemporary religious songbooks, such as *Songs of Praise*.)

2. Several days before the service, recruit students to fill the following roles:
- two readers for two short biblical readings (Matt. 7:7 and 7:8)
- one knocker and one reader for the dramatic reading on handout 4–A
- song leaders and, if available, instrumental accompanists for the song "Seek Ye First"

Provide these students with the materials that correspond with their part of the service and help them practice in advance. Also, review your parts of the service as leader.

3. A day before the service, inform the entire class of the upcoming prayer service and ask your students to prepare to participate in it by doing a homework assignment.

Ask the class to read, or review, the section "Please, God . . ." in the student text, pages 51–52. Tell the students to write a prayer of petition they would feel comfortable sharing with the class. Advise them to bring their prayer to class and to be prepared to offer their prayer aloud during the prayer service. (Also prepare a prayer of your own to offer during the service as an example.)

Suggest that the students also write at least three private prayers of petition in their reflection notebook. Stress that these prayers are for their own personal use and will be offered only as silent prayers during the service.

4

Procedure

Gathering: Invite the students to gather in a circle. Make sure they have their prayer of petition with them and ready to share. Sing the first verse of the song "Seek Ye First."

First reading: Pause for a moment or two after the song, then give the cue for the first biblical reading: "Ask, and it will be given you; search, and you will find; knock, and the door will be opened for you" (Matt. 7:7).

Ask: Give each student a pipe cleaner and say to the gathering:
- Jesus tells us to ask for what we need and it will be given to us. To do this, we must first understand two things: God's tremendous love and concern for us, and our dependence on God for every part of our life. When we know these two things in our heart, we can trustingly ask God for any need.

Then, offer these instructions:
- Let's each take a moment to call to mind a need or concern we would like to bring to God's attention. Think of a symbol to represent your prayer, and then shape the symbol with your pipe cleaner. When you are ready, silently come forward and place the symbol on the floor in the center of the prayer space.

When each person has placed a symbol on the floor, say,
- We spread these symbols out on the floor in front of us as a visual reminder of the variety of needs we can bring before God in petition.

Seek: Invite the students to share their prayer of petition with the group in the following manner:
- Jesus assures us that if we search for what we need, we will find it. At this time, I invite each of you to share your prayer of petition with the group. It's okay if your prayer is similar to someone else's. After each prayer, we will all respond, "God, we seek your help in our time of need." I will begin. *[Offer a prayer of your own.]*

After everyone in the circle has shared their prayer, offer this last petition:
- God, grant that we may find all that we seek, especially the prayers we have shared with one another today, the unspoken prayers written in our notebook, and those we still hold in our heart.

Ask everyone to respond, "God, we seek your help in our time of need."

Knock: Pause for a moment. Then, with these words, signal the students who will do the dramatic reading from handout 4–A to begin:

- Jesus also told us, "Knock, and the door will be opened for you."

Second reading: The second biblical reading should flow directly after the reading from handout 4–A: "For everyone who asks receives, and everyone who searches finds, and for everyone who knocks, the door will be opened" (Matt. 7:8).

Closing: Close by singing the second verse of "Seek Ye First."

Dial 911 for God

This discussion activity is designed to heighten students' awareness that God is always there for them and to encourage them to turn to God in prayer in times of need.

Begin the discussion by describing the following situation to the class:

- Once, when giving a retreat talk, a high school student said we should not think of God as a 911 God—someone we go to only in times of emergency. Some of the other young people at the retreat questioned the speaker on her views. They wondered if she meant that we should not turn to God when we are in trouble and then forget about God the rest of the time. If that was what she meant, they agreed. But, these other young people said, they did not see anything wrong with going to God when we are most in need. They pointed out that when we dial 911 for God, we know that the line is always open and that God will never hang up on us.

Then, conduct a period of discussion focused around questions such as these:

- How would you respond to someone who said we should not think of God as a 911 God?
- What kinds of needs should we ask for God's help with? What kinds of needs should we handle on our own?
- Why might people get stuck calling on God only when they are in trouble? What would you suggest to help them develop a fuller relationship with God?
- Can you think of any reason why someone might be reluctant to dial 911 for God in a time of great need?
- Do you feel comfortable dialing God for help? Why or why not?

Common-Object Prayers

This activity uses common objects found in any classroom as a springboard for prayers of petition, and creates a fun, light atmosphere for the students to become comfortable with prayers of petition.

Arrange the room so that the students' desks form a circle around a center table. Collect a dozen different objects commonly found in the classroom: an eraser, ruled paper, a pencil, chalk, a ruler, scissors, a pencil sharpener, a calculator, a globe, and so forth. Place the objects on the center table.

Challenge the students to use their imagination and to write twelve prayers of petition, each using a different object on the table as a starting point. They should focus especially on the object's symbolism. Let them know that their twelve prayers do not have to be about their own needs. They may write prayers for their class as a whole, their community, or any other group and for any nonpersonal concern. Offer some examples to get them started, such as these:

- *[Using an eraser]* God, help us to erase our mistakes and start fresh.
- *[Using a scissors]* God, help us to cut out our bad habits.
- *[Using a calculator]* God, help us to count our many blessings each day.

Give the students 15 minutes to develop their prayers. Then let the students share some of their prayers with the rest of the class, making sure this sharing covers all the objects.

Variation: Ask your students to bring an object from home and to write a prayer based on that object. Challenge them to be as creative as possible in their choice of object and in their prayer. Then, ask them to share their object and their prayer with the class.

Section B: How Does God Answer Prayers?

This section of the chapter in the student text, pages 53–58, asks students to recognize that God answers prayers in many ways, sometimes in ways we do not expect. It also explains that we can take an active role in working with God to find the answers to our prayers, and that using a discernment process can help us understand God's will for us.

Prayer Is a Two-Way Street

This personal reflection exercise helps students focus on prayer as an interactive process between ourselves and God.

Instruct the students to read the sections "How Does God Answer Prayers?" and "God's Will and Human Freedom" in their text, pages 53–55. Then assign handout 4–B, "Prayer Is a Two-Way Street," for in-class reflection or for homework.

Handout 4–B

Because of the personal nature of the handout questions and directives, students are instructed to record their responses in their reflection notebook, rather than on the handout. Assure your students that their responses will not be shared with the class.

Variation: Also ask several students to make a "Prayer Is a Two-Way Street" poster to hang in your classroom.

Making Decisions

This discussion and reflection activity corresponds directly to the section "Discernment: Seeking God's Will in Decisions" in the student text, pages 56–57. Use the activity to encourage your students to involve God and prayer in their decision-making process.

1. Assign the section "Discernment: Seeking God's Will in Decisions" as homework prior to this discussion.

2. Begin the discussion by asking your students to brainstorm different kinds of decisions they face right now. Record their responses on the board and elicit a list of at least twenty items. Remind the students that during a brainstorming session, all answers are valid, and that brainstorming involves only the sharing of ideas, no discussion. If needed, offer some examples to get things started:
- where to go to college
- which group of friends to hang out with
- whether or not to experiment with drugs

Once the list is formed, affirm that many of these decisions are faced by all of us. We are often not alone in the choices we have to make.

3. Ask the students to share some of the ways they make decisions. Record their responses on the board, and continue the sharing until at least ten ideas are listed. Again, offer some examples as starters:
- asking someone for advice
- listing the pros and cons
- flipping a coin

4. Introduce the term *discernment* and explain that it can be a way of bringing God and prayer into the decision-making process.

Go through the seven steps for discernment suggested by John Baptist de La Salle, found on pages 56–57 in the student text. Use some of the examples from your class's brainstormed list of decisions to help illustrate each step, and allow for comments or questions from the students. After the discussion of each step, give the students a few minutes to apply the step to a decision they currently face. Instruct them to write their response in their reflection notebook.

5. Conclude with a discussion in which the students compare De La Salle's discernment method for making decisions with some of the ways they listed earlier. Draw out the main point that discernment combines the best decision-making skills with an openness to God's will.

Voting for a Different Way

This activity shows students that the discernment process can be used by groups, as well as individuals, to make decisions that reflect God's will. The activity is best used as a follow-up to the preceding activity in this manual, "Making Decisions," and gives students more practice applying the discernment process.

1. Introduce the activity with comments similar to the following:
- All of us have opportunities to participate in making group decisions on a regular basis—in our family, at school, and in our community. The question Christians must ask is, How can we involve God in these decisions, as well as in our personal decisions? This activity shows us how groups, as well as individuals, can use the discernment process to make decisions that reflect God's will. The example we will be working with for this activity is our school's student council election.

2. Ask the students to describe the current decision-making process used for electing student council members. Make sure the students describe both the formal and informal aspects of the process. Briefly outline the process on the board. Then call for a quick evaluation of the process's strengths and weaknesses. Offer some examples if needed:

- A strength might be that the process tries to involve everyone at the school. A weakness might be that it ends up being simply a popularity contest.

3. Ask the students to describe, in their own words, the process of discernment. Review, if needed, the steps outlined on pages 56–57 of the student text, and record the students' comments on the board.

4. Pose the following question:

- How can we, as a school community, involve God in our decision-making process to elect student council members? In other words, how does discernment fit into this election process?

Go through each step of the discernment process and invite the students to offer ideas or suggestions in answer to this question. Wrap up the discussion by encouraging the students to use the discernment process the next time they participate in a group decision.

New Life Through Loss

This activity shows students how to recognize the ways God's grace and wisdom are active in their life, even during times of suffering or loss.

1. As homework prior to this session, ask your students to write in their reflection notebook about a situation of suffering or loss in their own life and about any good thing that came from that situation. Tell the students to then find or make a symbol that represents the new life that came from this loss, and to bring the symbol to class.

Inform the students that they will be asked to share their story in a small group and that the group will be making a collage with its symbols.

2. Divide the class into small groups of four or five. Distribute a piece of poster board, glue, and a set of large colored markers to each small group.

3. Give the groups about 15 to 20 minutes to share their stories and make their collage. Tell the groups to label their collage "New Life Through Loss." Hang the finished posters up around the room after the discussion time.

Variation: Invite one or more guest speakers to share with your students how, through a loss of some sort, they experienced new life. Possible guest speakers include the following:

- someone who received a transplant from an accident victim
- a parent who has a child with a learning disability
- a person who lost a parent to illness at an early age

Allow plenty of time for your students to ask questions of the speaker or speakers.

Section C:
Loving Others Through Intercessory Prayer

Pages 59–62 of the student text highlight a powerful way of showing our love for others, prayers of intercession. Through prayers of intercession we ask God to help another person, and in the process we invite God's loving presence into our relationship with that person. Our prayers of intercession can include those who have hurt us or who are in conflict with us. Bringing God into such relationships is an important step toward healing those relationships.

4

Prayer Partners

This prayer exchange invites students to recognize two things: first, that we have a responsibility to pray for one another, and second, that we need the prayers of others.

1. Prepare for this activity by writing the name of each person in the class on a slip of paper and putting the slips in a brown paper bag.

2. In class, begin by saying something like the following:
- When we care about someone, we often seek ways to let them know. We buy them a present for Christmas, surprise them with a party on their birthday, or give them a hug or a pat on the back. Another way we can show someone we care about them is by praying for them.

Explain to the students that they will be drawing one another's names and that the person whose name they draw will be their secret prayer partner for one week. (Decide ahead of time if you want to use the five-day school week or the seven-day calendar week. In either case, make sure the last day of your designated week is a class day.)

3. Pass the brown paper bag around and ask each student to draw a name. If someone draws their own name, have them put the slip of paper back in the bag and select another. Stress to the students that they are not to reveal the name of their prayer partner to anyone else—especially to that person.

4. Encourage the students to make a conscious effort to pray for their prayer partner by name every day for the duration. Suggest some ways they might pray for one another, such as in their morning or evening prayers, by dedicating their Sunday liturgy to their prayer partner, by reading a part of the Bible every day, and so forth. Whether their prayer is formal or informal, the important thing is to remember to pray for their prayer partner each day.

5. At the end of the week, let the students reveal their prayer partners in class.

Variation 1: If you will be concluding the class's work on this chapter with the "Ask. Seek. Knock." prayer service in this manual, pages 44–46, complete steps 1 to 4 of the "Prayer Partners" activity during the week before the service, and then invite the prayer partners to reveal themselves during a sign of peace added to the service.

Variation 2: Instead of arranging for prayer partners, give a slip of white paper to each student. Tell the students to write on their slip of paper the name of a person they do not get along with, they dislike, or they even hate. Then ask them to pray for this person for a week. At the end of the week, instruct the students to write in their reflection notebook how it felt to pray for an "enemy."

Prayer Through Action

By combining intercessory prayer with community service, this activity gives students the opportunity to widen their circle of concern beyond their family and friends.

1. Contact the local diocesan offices and ask to speak to the person who coordinates pregnancy support services for mothers-to-be in crisis. Some dioceses have homes, called Madonna Homes, and others offer outreach support.
    Invite the coordinator to visit your class and explain the program—how it is set up, the needs of the women and babies, and perhaps a general profile of the type of women who come to the agency for help. Also obtain from the coordinator a specific list of materials needed by the women and babies, such as clothes, formula, diapers, and toys. Distribute this list to the class and ask the students each to donate one or more of the items on it, to be collected later.

2. Give each student the initials of one mother-to-be from the support program. (To protect the privacy of the mothers, do not ask for names.) Ask the students to pray for the women, either individually or as a class. Request that the coordinator inform the women involved in the program that the class is praying for them.

3. After a few weeks or a month, collect the donated items from your students and ask the agency coordinator to pass these gifts along to the mothers-to-be.

Variation: Develop a similar activity around another social help program, such as a food pantry or a homeless shelter, in place of or in addition to the one for mothers-to-be.

4

Section D: The Communion of Saints

Pages 63–66 of the student text introduce the communion of saints—the union between the saints of history; our loved ones who have died; and ourselves, the living who are trying to do God's will. Praying with the communion of saints is a way of lifting up the prayers of the community to God.

Litany of the Saints

This activity introduces a beautiful and traditional prayer of the church, the Litany of the Saints. It gives students the opportunity to discover that saints are not just people put on a pedestal—figuratively or literally—but real people with whom we can unite in prayer.

Handout 4–C

Ask each student to name any special intention or person for whom she or he would like to pray. Distribute handout 4–C, "Litany of the Saints," to the class and invite the students to pray the litany together.

Variation: Invite the students to add the names of deceased loved ones onto the end of the first part of the litany, asking these loved ones to pray for us as well.

4

"Knock . . ."

Knocker: *[Knock, knock, knock]*
Reader: Come in, with your dreams.

Knocker: *[Knock, knock, knock]*
Reader: Enter, carrying your wishes and your longings.

Knocker: *[Knock, knock, knock]*
Reader: Open the door, you who are afraid or worried, or weighed down.

Knocker: *[Knock, knock, knock]*
Reader: Bring your dreams, bring your hopes, bring your burdens.

Knocker: *[Knock, knock, knock]*
Reader: Bring them all here to be blessed and made holy.

Knocker: *[Knock, knock, knock]*
Reader: Bring them to me because they are *you.*

Knocker: *[Knock, knock, knock]*
Reader: Welcome. Be at home. Come in.

Prayer Is a Two-Way Street

Write your responses to the following questions and directives in your reflection notebook:

1. Describe a time when you prayed for something but did not seem to get a response.

2. Describe a time when God answered your prayer but in a way you did not expect.

3. Write a prayer for a need you have right now.

4. How can you take action with God to meet this need?

5. How might God respond to your prayer?

Litany of the Saints

Leader	Respondents
Lord, have mercy	Lord, have mercy
Christ, have mercy	Christ, have mercy
Lord, have mercy	Lord, have mercy
Holy Mary, Mother of God	pray for us
Saint Michael	pray for us
Holy angels of God	pray for us
Saint John the Baptist	pray for us
Saint Joseph	pray for us
Saint Peter and Saint Paul	pray for us
Saint Andrew	pray for us
Saint John	pray for us
Saint Mary Magdalene	pray for us
Saint Stephen	pray for us
Saint Ignatius	pray for us
Saint Lawrence	pray for us
Saint Perpetua and Saint Felicity	pray for us
Saint Agnes	pray for us
Saint Gregory	pray for us
Saint Augustine	pray for us
Saint Athanasius	pray for us
Saint Basil	pray for us
Saint Martin	pray for us
Saint Benedict	pray for us
Saint Francis and Saint Dominic	pray for us
Saint Francis Xavier	pray for us
Saint John Vianney	pray for us
Saint Catherine	pray for us
Saint Teresa	pray for us
All holy men and women	pray for us
Lord, be merciful	Lord, save your people
From all evil	Lord, save your people
From every sin	Lord, save your people
From everlasting death	Lord, save your people
By your coming as man	Lord, save your people
By your death and rising to new life	Lord, save your people
By your gift of the Holy Spirit	Lord, save your people
Be merciful to us sinners	Lord, hear our prayer

CHAPTER 5

Thanks and Praise:
Giving God a Joyful Heart

Section A: All Is a Gift

The beginning section of this chapter in the student text, pages 67–73, invites students to see every aspect of life as a gift from God. Cultivating the virtue of humility is the best way to recognize the giftedness of life. However, humility stands in sharp contrast to the approach to life promoted by the dominant culture, an approach characterized by a worship of independence and self-centeredness.

Eye-Opening Experiences

This reflection and discussion encourages students to share stories of crises and life-changing events that resulted in a sense of wonder and gratitude for the way God works.

1. Begin this activity by placing an alarm clock on a desk or table and allowing it to ring, beep, or buzz for 10 to 15 seconds. Then say something similar to the following:
   - Alarm clocks are not pleasant. They disturb us from our sleep. Rarely do we look forward to having them go off in the morning. Yet, for many of us, they are essential. Without them our days would consistently get off to a late start!

     Some life experiences, such as the one described at the beginning of chapter 5 in your textbook, are a lot like alarm clocks. They wake us up and call us to take a hard look at what is really important in our life.

2. Instruct your students to spend a few minutes thinking about a time when they or someone they know experienced one of these wake-up calls, and about how this experience changed them or the other person.

3. After 3 to 5 minutes, divide the class into small groups of three and ask the students to share their story with their group.

Variation: In steps 2 and 3, ask the students to think about wake-up call stories they read in the paper or heard on television or the radio, and to relate them to the whole class.

56

🌳 Half Empty or Half Full?

This day-by-day reflection builds on the story of the ocean fish on page 70 of the student text, and challenges students to look beyond the obvious to see God's goodness in everyday happenings.

1. Place a clear glass filled halfway with colored water on a desk in the front of the room. Tell the students to write a description of the object on the desk, and to do so without consulting one another.

2. After a few minutes, call for several volunteers to describe what they see. Then take a poll to see how many students described the glass as half full and how many described the glass as half empty.

3. In their reflection notebook, have your students date three pages, beginning with today's date, and draw a line down the middle of each page, labeling one column "Blessings" and the other "Burdens." Ask the students to spend a few minutes in the evening of each of the three days thinking about all the things that happened to them during the day, and to list those things under the appropriate column. Encourage the students to make a special effort to look for the blessings in their day.

4. After the students have recorded their blessings and burdens for three days, allow class time for them to share with a partner the answers to these questions, which you have written on the board:
   • Which column contained the most items?
   • What are some of the blessings you encountered in the past three days?
   • What are some of the burdens you encountered in the past three days?
   • Did you find it easier to see the burdens or the blessings?
   • Might the burdens of life actually be blessings?
   • What can you do to help yourself and others see life as half full rather than half empty?

5. Close this activity by encouraging the students to actively look for the blessings in their life.

🌳 God, Yet a Humble Man

This Scripture-based discussion lets students discover, in Jesus, the kind of humility needed to see all life as a gift.

Ask a student to read Mark 1:32–43 to the class. Lead a large-group discussion focused on the following questions:
   • Does the way Jesus deals with his popularity surprise you? How would you expect a person to deal with such popularity?
   • How do Jesus' actions in this Gospel passage compare with the description of humility on pages 72–73 in your textbook?
   • How does Jesus' example of humility, or your textbook's definition, compare with your own understanding of humility?
   • Why does seeing the giftedness of life require an attitude of humility?

Praise God Through Others

This affirmation exercise recognizes that one of the best ways to praise God is through praising and affirming the people God has given to us. This exercise continues throughout the entire time the class works with chapter 5.

1. Ask each student to bring to class an empty quart-size plastic jar (such as a peanut butter jar), with no lid, labeled with the student's name in large, easy-to-read block letters. Place the jars in a prominent place, such as along a windowsill or on a side table, where they can remain undisturbed for the period of time the class works on this chapter.

2. Inform the students that these are "care jars." Tell them that at the beginning of each class period while they are working on chapter 5, they will have the opportunity to write something positive and affirming to several classmates. They are to write each affirmation on a piece of notepaper, and then fold the piece of paper over and write the intended person's name on the front. You will collect the notes, and after class you will place each one in the intended person's jar. The notes may be signed or left anonymous.

3. Distribute a list of all the class members. Suggest that when the students write a note to a person, they cross that person's name off their list. Explain that this will help them make sure that, over time, they write a note to each person in the class.

Also emphasize that the contents of the jars are to remain private—no one is permitted to take notes out of a jar to read, until instructed to—and that the messages are to be positive and affirming.

4. Pass out small pieces of notepaper and give the students a few minutes to write their first notes. Collect the notes and then proceed with your other planned activities. After the students have been dismissed for the day, place the notes in the appropriate jars.

5. At the end of the class's work on this chapter, give each student her or his care jar. Suggest that the students find a quiet time at home to read the notes. They might want to store their care jar in a special place so that they can look over the notes again sometime when they are feeling down and in need of something to lift their spirit.

Section B: A Grateful, Praise-Filled People

Pages 73–75 of the student text look at the tradition of praise and gratitude in Christian prayer, beginning with the psalms of the ancient Jews. The early Christians continued this tradition, and found the ultimate expression of praise and gratitude to be their celebration of the Eucharist.

Different Ways to Praise

This activity examines the many ways to praise God through music. It explores the richness and diversity found in the church throughout history, and in different cultures.

1. Introduce the activity with comments such as these:
- Music is an important part of most cultures, especially in religious traditions. In fact, the often-repeated saying "He (or she) who sings, prays twice" comes from a long-held belief that music is a beautiful way to praise God. The psalms of the Hebrew Scriptures were the ancient Israelites' way of giving glory to God for life's blessings. Hymns have played a central part in worship throughout the history of the Christian church. In this activity, we will take some time to look more closely at music that praises or can be used to praise God.

2. Divide the class into pairs and assign one of the following categories to each pair:
- psalm (not Psalm 104, which is used in the student text)
- Gregorian chant
- ethnic song or hymn (in English, or in another language if the English translation is available)
- traditional church hymn (Latin or English)
- contemporary church song (written in the last twenty years)
- Top 40 song (playing currently on the radio)
- Christian rock song

If the class is large, add more categories or assign the same category to two or more pairs.

3. Tell each pair to find an example for its assigned category and to prepare a 5-minute class presentation on it. The presentation should include playing or performing a portion of the selection and sharing with the class the pair's ideas on how the selection praises God.

Variation 1: Invite the pairs to update a traditional psalm of praise by rewriting it using contemporary language. Ask the pairs to share with the class the original version of the psalm and their revised version.

Variation 2: Ask the pairs to match a psalm of praise with a contemporary song that has a similar message and to share both with the class.

5

The Eucharist as Praise

This activity encourages students to explore the Eucharist as a prayer of thanksgiving.

Handout 5–A

Inform the students that they will be examining the eucharistic celebration to identify prayers and parts of the liturgy that praise and thank God. Pass out missalettes that include all parts of the Mass, and handout 5–A, "The Eucharist as Praise." Tell the students to follow the instructions given on the handout. This activity may be done in class or as a home assignment.

Section C: Growing in Gratitude

This section of the chapter in the student text, pages 76–81, encourages students to wake up to the surprises all around them and to treasure the gift of life in all circumstances. It acknowledges that the real challenge is finding something to be thankful for in times of pain and suffering, but explains that God can and does bring forth life from death. The Resurrection of Jesus witnesses this truth. Examples in this section of the text show that a heart truly grateful for God's love can experience joy in even the toughest times.

Surprise!

This activity involves surprising students with a small gift as a way to encourage them to look for surprises in their everyday life.

Gather the following materials:
- a book of spiritual or contemporary quotations
- blank slips of paper
- a small box (such as a paper clip box) for each member of the class
- transparent tape
- a scissors
- wrapping paper (Sunday comics from the newspaper are a colorful and inexpensive substitute for regular wrapping paper.)

Identify quotations or words of wisdom that include the word *surprise,* and write a different one on each slip of paper. Place a quotation slip inside each box and wrap the box.

Before the students arrive for class on the day you will be dealing with this part of the chapter, place a box on each student's desk. Let the students open their box. Encourage them to look for the many hidden surprises in their life—that is, the surprises beyond those that arrive on birthdays or come wrapped in plain view on their desk. Stress that surprise is more than a word we yell as we jump out of the dark when someone walks into the room for a party they did not know about. Invite the students to expand their notion of a surprise and to look at all of God's creation with wonder and surprise.

Variation: Write a saying such as "Surprise! God loves you!" or "Every day is a new surprise" on a helium balloon, and put the balloon in a large box. Wrap the box and place it in the center of the room. Either let the students open the box at the beginning of class, or pique their curiosity and make them wait until the end of class to open the box.

And Now for Something Totally Different

This activity uses changes in class setting and routine to show students how surprise and change can help us "wake up" to the things in life we may take for granted.

Use your own ideas or any of the following suggestions to surprise your students by changing the setting of the classroom and the class routine:

- Prior to the students' arrival, turn all the desks to face a different direction, such as all looking out the window or all facing one another in two rows.
- If the students have assigned seats, change the order by asking all those who sit in the front to move to the back, or all those who sit by the door to sit by the window.
- If it is a nice day, move the entire class outside under a tree.
- If you usually take attendance at the beginning of class, do it at the end.
- Switch the opening and closing prayers.
- If you review at the end of the class everyday, do so at the beginning.
- Assign homework in the middle of class instead of at the end.

Follow up the changes with a general discussion about surprises, based on questions such as these:

- Do you like being surprised? Why or why not?
- What was your favorite surprise ever?
- How were you surprised by what we did today?
- What are some of the little surprises you encountered in the last week?
- What do you need to help you "wake up" to the surprises God has given to you?

Caring for the Gift

This out-of-class group assignment encourages students to care for the gift of creation through environmental service work.

Introduce this assignment with the following words:

- A great way to show gratitude for the gifts God has given us is to take care of those gifts. If we are given something precious, we do not throw it in a corner under a pile of clothes. We put it in a keepsake box where it can be protected, or in a place of honor where it can be admired. This attitude of care applies to all God's gifts to us, including the gift of creation.

Brainstorm with the students on projects they could do, as a class, to take care of the environment. Offer some suggestions, such as setting up a school recycling effort or joining the Adopt-a-Highway cleanup program.

For other ideas, contact a local environmental awareness group.

Variation: Invite someone from a local environmental awareness group to come talk to the class and to help the class get involved in an environmental service project.

5

🌲 Looking Back on the Road of Life

This reflection asks students to look back on some of the toughest times in their life and discover the gifts found in suffering.

Introduce the assignment by saying something similar to the following:

- One of the toughest places to find room for gratitude is in the midst of suffering. It is only human for us to feel like blaming God, rather than thanking God, for what has befallen us or our friends or family. Perhaps that is why we often need to step back from a situation and look back on it from down the road a distance before we can see the blessings of the situation.

Handout 5–B

Assign handout 5–B, "Looking Back on the Road of Life," for home reflection this evening. Let the students know that what they write on the handout will not be shared in class, so they can be open and honest with their feelings. Inform them that, however, they will be asked to hand in their completed handout at the beginning of the next class. Suggest that they refer to the examples on pages 78–79 in their textbook for ideas. Also mention that instead of writing about themselves, they may write about a friend or someone in their family, parish, or workplace who has struggled through, and survived, a really tough period.

Caution: You may want to avoid using this activity if the school or someone in the class has just suffered a serious loss. It may be unrealistic to expect someone to find any good or blessing when they are beginning or in the midst of the grieving process.

🌲 An Experience of Joy

This assignment helps students experience the power of joy through the storytelling of others.

Tell your students that their assignment is to interview someone they know who has experienced joy. Offer the following examples to show students the wide range of events in which a person might experience joy:

- a person who won a long-sought-after medal in a sporting event
- a firefighter who rescued someone from a fire
- a woman who recently gave birth
- a newly married couple
- a person who was reunited with a family member after a long separation
- a parent whose baby recently took his or her first steps, or said his or her first words
- a pilot who just completed her or his first solo flight
- a newly ordained minister
- a person who has overcome a serious health problem

Stress that the students are not limited to these examples for their interviews.

Handout 5–C

Distribute handout 5–C, "Tell Me About a Joyful Experience." Instruct the students to use the handout as a guide for their interview and to record their interview on it.

Variation: Ask the students to write in their reflection notebook about some of their own joyful experiences. Let them know that the experiences can be dramatic, like those described in their textbook, or quite simple, such as these:

- passing your driver's test
- acing a tough test in school
- getting the date you wanted for the prom
- having an unexpected day off school
- being accepted by the college you dreamed of going to
- finding a much-loved pet who was lost

Thank You, God

This activity urges students to reflect on their new understanding of praise and thanksgiving and offers them a means to express it through writing. It is a good way to draw this chapter to a close.

Distribute thank-you notes and envelopes. Invite your students to take some reflection time to write a personal thank-you note to God. The notes can be about anything the students wish to thank God for.

Insist that all be quiet during this reflection time. If possible, spread out in the school chapel or library, where the students can be comfortable.

Advise the students to seal their note in the envelope when they have finished writing, and to put their name on the envelope. Collect the notes in a basket. Tell the students their notes will be placed in front of the Blessed Sacrament in the chapel, and then returned to them unopened at the end of the quarter or semester.

5

The Eucharist as Praise

Examine all the parts of the Eucharist in the missalette. Using the spaces provided on this handout, identify and discuss three prayers or parts of the liturgy that praise and thank God.

Example 1

Prayer or part of the liturgy:

Excerpts of the prayer or of the part of the liturgy:

How does this prayer or part of the liturgy help us praise and thank God?

Example 2

Prayer or part of the liturgy:

Excerpts of the prayer or of the part of the liturgy:

How does this prayer or part of the liturgy help us praise and thank God?

Example 3

Prayer or part of the liturgy:

Excerpts of the prayer or of the part of the liturgy:

How does this prayer or part of the liturgy help us praise and thank God?

Handout 5–A: Permission to reproduce this handout for classroom use is granted.

Looking Back on the Road of Life

"Give thanks in all circumstances." (1 Thessalonians 5:18)

Complete the following statements in the spaces provided:

4. Other people helped me
get through it by . . .

_____

_____

_____

_____

2. When this happened,
I felt . . .

_____

_____

_____

_____

5. This time may have been
a blessing in disguise
because . . .

_____

_____

_____

_____

3. God helped me get
through this time by . . .

_____

_____

_____

_____

1. A time when suffering
touched my life was . . .

_____

_____

_____

_____

Tell Me About a Joyful Experience

Base your interview on the following questions. Record the interview directly on this handout or in your reflection notebook.

1. Please describe a situation in which you experienced joy.

2. Is there a special reason that this experience was joyful for you? If so, what?

3. Did this joyful experience change your life in any way? If so, how?

4. Do you feel that God was working in this experience? Please explain.

5. Did you thank God for this experience? If so, how?

CHAPTER 6

Journal Writing:
A Conversation with God

Section A: Journal Writing About One's Life

The opening section of chapter 6 in the student text, pages 83–87, advocates using a personal journal to maintain an ongoing conversation with God. Journal writing is a way to record our experiences, and a tool for reflecting on and understanding those experiences. It also helps us learn more about ourselves and offers us a place to work through our problems.

Journals for Life

Students in this course already have some experience with journal writing because of their work with their reflection notebook. The purpose of this chapter is to encourage students to make journal writing a regular part of their life and their prayer.

The following activities let students explore some of the many ways journal writing can help them understand themselves and their life. Directly communicate these activities to your students as written here. The students may do all these activities in their reflection notebook.

The Invisible Journal Writer

- If you could be invisible for two hours, what would you do during that time? Why?

Trading Places

- If you could trade places with anyone in the world for one day, who would it be? Why? What would you do? Why? Would you be glad to return to being you? Why or why not?

Travel by Pen

- In your mind, go to your favorite place in the entire world. Describe it in your journal. What does it look like? What do you see? What sounds and smells are around you? What do you feel when you are in this place? Why is this your favorite place?

67

Playing in the Sand

- If you were sitting on a sandy beach, with all the time in the world, what would you build in the sand? Why? If you want to, sketch your sand creation in your journal.

Dear President

- Write a letter to the president of the United States. What key social problem would you like the president to take action on—homelessness, abortion, violence, poverty, or some other issue? What key world problem would you like the president to look into—famine in Africa, unrest in the Middle East, global neglect of the environment, or some other situation?

Time Travel

- Imagine yourself ten years from now. What will you be doing? Where will you be living? How will your life have changed? What will you have accomplished? How will you have made a difference in the life of others?

Section B: Prayer and the Journal

Journal writing can open the door for us to pray daily and to discover God's presence, according to pages 88–90 in the student text. By bringing our day to God in prayer, we invite God to be part of our experiences.

Journals for Prayer

Teaching activity suggestions for previous chapters asked students to use their reflection notebook for prayerful reflection. The following exercises offer students more ideas on how to pray their experiences through journal writing. Directly communicate these activities to your students as written here. The students may do all these activities in their reflection notebook.

Dream Weaver

- Keep your reflection notebook by your bed. The next time you wake up after having a dream, write the dream down right away before you forget it. Later, when you are a little more awake, reflect on what you think God may have tried to tell you in your dream.

Messages in the Music

- Write the words to your favorite song in your journal, then play a tape or CD of the song as you read the words. What does the song say to you? Highlight a few of the lines and make a connection to where you are in your life right now. Do you feel as if you could have written this song or as if it was written for you? If so, why? What might God be trying to say to you through your attraction to this song?

On the Last Day

- If you found out you had only one more day to live, how would you spend it? Describe the entire twenty-four hours in as much detail as possible. Why would you spend your last day in this way?

Weeding the Garden

- What is growing in the garden of your life—flowers? vegetables? exotic plants? trees and bushes? weeds? What seeds do you want to plant? What weeds do you have to pull out?

Words of Wisdom

- Reserve a few pages in the back of your journal and label them "Words of Wisdom." Whenever you hear or read a quote you want to remember, jot it down in this section of your journal, along with some comments on what the quote means to you.

Homily Collection

- If you hear a homily at Mass that you really like or that seems to relate directly to where you are at right now, summarize the message in your journal when you get home. Add your own reflections or insights gained from the homily.

    If you hear a homily that you do not like or that you disagree with, summarize it in your journal. Then write about what you found wrong with it and what you would have said instead.

Interview of a Lifetime

- Imagine you are a reporter and your editor just gave you the assignment of your life: you are going to interview Jesus Christ. You are allowed to ask only five questions. Write your five questions in your journal, along with how you think Jesus would answer them.

6

Section C: Keeping a Journal

The major portion of this chapter in the student text, pages 90–98, offers practical suggestions for writing in a journal and discusses a number of basic techniques of journal writing. It also includes a number of specific activities students can do in order to practice some of the suggestions and techniques discussed in their text.

Using the Text Activities

To help your students get the most out of the activities offered on pages 92–97 in their text, carefully review those activities before assigning this section of the chapter, and decide the best way to work with each activity. For example, some activities could be assigned along with the reading as homework, whereas others could be done during class. The students' reflection notebook is an appropriate place for them to do these activities.

More Journal-Writing Ideas

The following additional ideas allow students to gain more experience and confidence in using a journal. Some exercises are to be assigned verbally and can be done in the students' reflection notebook; others are presented on a handout and summarized here for your review. For the handout activities, students may record their thoughts either directly on the handout or in their reflection notebook.

Review the following activities and decide which ones best fit your students' learning needs at this point in the course. Consider reserving some activities for use later in the course. Some could be offered to students at the conclusion of the course to encourage them to continue writing in their journal after the class ends.

Comic Relief

This activity lets students reflect on the value of laughter.

Have the students scan today's comic pages and cut out a comic that really made them laugh. They should paste the comic in their reflection notebook and answer the following questions:
- Why did it make you laugh?
- Why is it healthy to have a good laugh now and then?
- How do you make others laugh?

6

A Time for Everything

Handout 6–A

Handout 6–A, "A Time for Everything," uses the well-known passage "For everything there is a season . . ." (Eccles.3:1–8) to help students reflect on what things are appropriate for their life right now.

Taking off the Masks

Handout 6–B

Journal writing tends to help us be more honest with ourselves about who we truly are, because of the reflective nature of the task. Handout 6–B, "Taking Off the Masks," gives students the opportunity to examine how they present themselves to others—what masks they wear—and then who they really are.

A Prayer for Serenity

Handout 6–C

Handout 6–C, "A Prayer for Serenity," uses "The Serenity Prayer," by Protestant theologian Reinhold Niebuhr (1892–1971), as a springboard for reflection. Students are encouraged to cultivate their own inner wisdom by contemplating the aspects of their life they can change as well as those they cannot and must instead find the strength to accept.

On the Tube

This activity helps students develop the skill of critical reflection about the world around them.

Direct the students to watch an hour of prime-time television one night. They should spend some time "channel surfing" (switching to a different channel every few minutes) to get an idea of what is on all the channels. Then, they should list at least three of the shows they saw, and answer these questions:

- How much violence did you see?
- What values did the shows seem to be promoting?
- What were the commercials trying to sell?
- Did you find God anywhere?

You Have to Believe

Handout 6–D

Through a brief story, handout 6–D, "You Have to Believe," asks students to examine issues of self-confidence and belief in their abilities to accomplish what they want in life.

The Lord Is Kind and Merciful

This activity allows students to relate selected scriptural readings to their own experience.

Ask the student to read Psalm 103:1–4,9–12 and then respond to these questions:

- What does this psalm tell you about the mercy of God?
- What do you need God's forgiveness for right now?

Also ask them to read Matthew 5:7 and then respond to these questions:

- What does Jesus tell you about those who are merciful?
- Who do you need to forgive right now?

Doodle Here

Instruct your students to spend some time, either in class or for a home assignment, drawing a few simple doodles in their reflection notebook. Tell them to, when they are done, study the doodles for a while and then write a creative prayer for each one.

Variation: Conclude the activity by asking the students to share with the class one of their doodles and the prayer they wrote for it.

Answering a Letter

Handout 6–E

Handout 6–E, "Answering a Letter," lets students journey back in time to the beginnings of the Christian church. They are asked to imagine themselves as a first-century Christian from the Asia Minor city Colossae. The Christian community there has just received a letter from the Apostle Paul. The handout asks students to respond to a segment of Paul's letter.

Pennies in the Fountain

This activity encourages students to search their heart for their deepest wishes.

Tell the students to imagine they have five pennies to throw into a fountain, for five of their deepest wishes. They should list the five wishes and explain why each one is important to them. Then they should reflect on these two questions in their journal:

- What can you do to help your wishes come true?
- How can God help you make your wishes come true?

Newspaper Clippings

This activity asks students to respond to a disturbing newspaper story and to consider how Jesus would respond to it.

Direct the students to clip out from the newspaper a story that really disturbs them and tape it in their reflection notebook. Below the clipping, they should explain why they find the story disturbing and then describe how Jesus might respond to the story.

Saying Yes to God and Others

Handout 6–F

The poem "Saying Yes to God and His People," by William F. McKee, offers students food for thought in handout 6–F, "Saying Yes to God and Others." Students are asked to reflect on the many ways they can respond positively to God and God's people.

What Now?

Handout 6–G

Handout 6–G, "What Now?" contains an illustration in which a person is surrounded by a group of thugs. Students are asked to put themselves in the person's shoes and write about how they would respond to the situation. They are also asked to describe how they might respond if they put on the heart and mind of Jesus.

I Am No Longer a Child

Handout 6–H

Through a prayer poem, handout 6–H, "I Am No Longer a Child," encourages students to express their feelings about the hardships and benefits of growing up, and to ask God's help in that process.

6

A Time for Everything

Read this scriptural passage and respond to the reflection questions and directives that follow it:

> For everything there is a season, and a time for every matter under heaven:
>   a time to be born, and a time to die;
>   a time to plant, and a time to pluck up what is planted;
>   a time to kill, and a time to heal;
>   a time to break down, and a time to build up;
>   a time to weep, and a time to laugh;
>   a time to mourn, and a time to dance;
>   a time to throw away stones, and a time to gather stones together;
>   a time to embrace, and a time to refrain from embracing;
>   a time to seek, and a time to lose;
>   a time to keep, and a time to throw away;
>   a time to tear, and a time to sew;
>   a time to keep silence, and a time to speak;
>   a time to love, and a time to hate;
>   a time for war, and a time for peace.

(Ecclesiastes 3:1–8)

For Reflection

- List some things for which now is the appropriate time in your life. Explain why you feel this way.

- Describe the hardest time in your life so far. Why was it so hard?

- Describe the best time in your life so far. Why was it so good?

Taking Off the Masks

Complete these statements and then respond to the reflection questions that follow them:

The masks I wear when I am with others are . . .

The real me is . . .

For Reflection

- Why is it sometimes hard to take off our masks and allow our true self to come through?

- Are there situations when it seems appropriate to put on a mask? If you think so, name several such situations and discuss why a mask is appropriate for them. If you think masks are never appropriate, explain why.

A Prayer for Serenity

Read this prayer and respond to the reflection questions that follow it:

The Serenity Prayer

God, give us grace to accept with serenity the things that cannot be changed, courage to change the things which should be changed, and the wisdom to distinguish the one from the other.
(Reinhold Niebuhr, in John Bartlett, *Familiar Quotations,* page 823)

For Reflection

- What things in your life right now do you need to change? Ask God for the courage to make those changes.

- What things in your life right now cannot be changed and are tough to accept? Ask God for the strength to accept what cannot be changed.

- How do you know which things to change and which to accept? What criteria do you use? What signs might help you decide? Ask God for the wisdom to make this decision.

Handout 6–C: Permission to reproduce this handout for classroom use is granted.

75

You Have to Believe

Read this story and respond to the reflection questions that follow it:

Believe It, Achieve It

In the "Star Wars" movie, *The Empire Strikes Back,* Luke Skywalker flies his X-wing ship to a swamp planet on a personal quest. There he seeks out a Jedi master named Yoda to teach him the ways of becoming a Jedi warrior. Luke wants to free the galaxy from the oppression of the evil tyrant, Darth Vader.

Yoda reluctantly agrees to help Luke and begins by teaching him how to lift rocks with his mental powers.

Then, one day, Yoda tells Luke to lift his ship out from the swamp where it sank after a crash landing. Luke complains that lifting rocks is one thing, but lifting a star-fighter is quite another matter. Yoda insists. Luke manages a valiant effort but fails in his attempt.

Yoda then focuses his mind, and lifts out the ship with ease. Luke, dismayed, exclaims, "I don't believe it!"

"That's why you couldn't lift it," Yoda replied. "You didn't believe you could."

(Mark Link, in Brian Cavanaugh, *More Sower's Seeds,* page 76)

For Reflection

- What are some things you would like to achieve?

- What do you need to believe in, in order to accomplish what you want in life?

- What are some areas in which you lack self-confidence?

- How can faith in God help you build faith in yourself?

- How can faith in God help you achieve your goals?

Answering a Letter

Imagine yourself as a first-century Christian from the Asia Minor city of Colossae. The Christian community in Colossae has just received a letter from the Apostle Paul. The following is a segment of that letter. Read it carefully and then write a letter back to Paul.

As God's chosen ones, holy and beloved, clothe yourselves with compassion, kindness, humility, meekness, and patience. Bear with one another and, if anyone has a complaint against another, forgive each other; just as the Lord has forgiven you, so you also must forgive. Above all, clothe yourselves with love, which binds everything together in perfect harmony. And let the peace of Christ rule in your hearts, to which indeed you were called in the one body. And be thankful. Let the word of Christ dwell in you richly; teach and admonish one another in all wisdom; and with gratitude in your hearts sing psalms, hymns, and spiritual songs to God. And whatever you do, in word or deed, do everything in the name of the Lord Jesus, giving thanks to God the Father through him. (Colossians 3:12–17)

Handout 6–E: Permission to reproduce this handout for classroom use is granted.

77

Saying Yes to God and Others

Read this poem, "Saying Yes to God and His People," and respond to the reflection questions that follow it:

Saying yes to God and his people is a good
    thing.

Saying yes to God is adoration.
It's awareness.
It's understanding.
It's prayer
It's reassurance.
It's faith.

Worry
Pain
Loss
Inhumanity
Betrayal
Sin
Lack of concern
Indifference

Horror
    tend to tie the yessing tongue.
Tied tongues can always be untied.

Peace
Grace
Glory
    follow.

People too need yesses.
All the time.
People need to know that they are
    worthwhile.
Yes reassures them.
People are weak.
Yes supplies strength.

Saying yes may be

    a nod
    a smile
    a tear
    a being there

    a hand
    a loving
    a walking with
    a talking to
    a listening
    a saying no.

Where people end and God begins is hard to see.
Ofttimes God and people are the same.

Dapple each day with yesses.
Greet morn and eve with a yes.

Saying yes is godliness.

(William F. McKee, *Listen with Your Heart,* pages 9–10; originally published in *Ligourian,* May 1985.
Reprinted with permission from *Ligourian,* One Liguori Drive, Liguori, MO 63057.)

〰〰〰〰〰〰〰〰〰 **For Reflection** 〰〰〰〰〰〰〰〰〰

• How can you say yes to God?

_____

_____

_____

_____

_____

_____

• How can you say yes to others?

_____

_____

_____

_____

_____

_____

     Handout 6–F: Permission to reproduce this handout for classroom use is granted.

What Now?

Imagine yourself in the predicament of the person in this illustration. You must decide, What am I going to do now? After studying the situation for a few moments, proceed with the reflection questions and directives following the illustration.

So it's gonna be a prayer group, huh?

For Reflection

• First write your gut response.

• Then write what you think the "logical" response should be.

• Finally, consider your response if you put on the heart and mind of Jesus and responded in the way you think Jesus would.

• How does this third response compare with the first two?

Handout 6–G: Permission to reproduce this handout for classroom use is granted.

79

I Am No Longer a Child

Read this prayer, at the same time imagining yourself as its author, and then respond to the reflection questions and directives that follow it:

> Living God,
> I am no longer a child.
> You will not do my work,
> play the game for me,
> fight my battles.
> So be it,
> as long as you cheer me on the way.
>   (William J. O'Malley, *Daily Prayers for Busy People*, page 86)

For Reflection

• What does growing up mean to you?

• What fears do you have about growing up?

• Do you welcome any aspects of growing up? If so, what are they?

• Write a prayer asking God's help as you grow into adulthood.

Handout 6–H: Permission to reproduce this handout for classroom use is granted.

CHAPTER 7

Meditation:
Dwelling on the Mystery of God

Section A: The Hunger for Meditation

The beginning of this chapter in the student text, pages 99–105, calls us to recognize that we all have a need for meditation, even if we cannot name that hunger. The dizzying speed of living in today's world increases the need to practice meditation, but meditation is a discipline that requires dedicated effort. Christian meditation centers on deepening our relationship with God. It can bring balance to our life, offer the comfort of healing, and enable us to live life to the full.

The Hunger Without a Name

This activity uses the video *Jingo* to help raise students' awareness that hunger is not just a physical feeling, but also can be experienced as a need for quiet and stillness. See appendix 2 for information on ordering the video.

Before showing the video, make sure everyone is seated where they can easily see the television screen. Show the video when everyone has settled in and quieted down.

Allow a few minutes of quiet reflection after viewing the video. Then lead a large-group discussion based on these or similar questions:
- What types of physical hunger did Jingo experience?
- What other hungers or needs did Jingo have?
- What is the hunger that does not have a name?
- How is this hunger different from the physical hunger for food? How is it similar?
- How can we satisfy this hunger?

Turn Down the Volume

This discussion asks students to look critically at the amount of quiet in their daily life and to see the need to make more time for quiet and reflection.

1. In preparation for this activity, do the following tasks:
- Borrow a sound meter from a music teacher, a local music store, or a sound studio.
- Arrange for the use of a meeting space away from the main classroom and administrative areas of the school.
- Set up a tape player or CD player with large speakers in the meeting space before class.
- Choose music that is loud and dissonant.
- On the day before the activity, inform your students that they are to gather at the arranged meeting space for the next day's class.

2. As the students enter the meeting space for class, play the selected music loudly enough so that they must strain to hear one another speak in their side conversations. After everyone is present, turn down the music so that it is playing only in the background.

3. Proceed with these words of introduction:
- We live in a very noisy world. In fact, noise pollution is a significant problem today. No matter where we are—at home, with friends, at work, or even in school—the air is overflowing with sound. We tend to fill in every space with music or conversation, or some kind of background noise. With all this auditory stimulus, it can sometimes be tough to hear our own thoughts—much less the people next to us! Yet very few of us ever think to turn down the volume. It's as if we are afraid of the quiet.

  During this discussion, I would like you to ponder the question How loud is my life?

4. Bring out the sound meter and explain that it is a device to measure the intensity of sound in decibels. Demonstrate that increasing the volume of the music increases the decibel level, and lowering the volume lowers the decibel level.

5. Ask your students to find a partner. Tell the pairs to discuss some of the noises and distractions they experience at home, at school, with friends, at work, and at some other setting of their choice. Write these categories on the board for easy reference. Ask the pairs to give a decibel rating for each category, using a range of 1 to 10, with 1 being the quietest and 10 being the loudest.

6. Close this discussion with a brainstorming session on some of the ways we can turn down the volume in our life. If needed, offer some examples to get things started:
- being respectful when someone else is trying to study
- not yelling at a younger brother or sister
- spending more time doing quiet things outdoors rather than sitting inside blasting the radio or television

Variation 1: Instead of conducting the final brainstorming session, encourage your students to spend some quiet time at home that evening reflecting on ways they can turn down the volume in their life, and to jot down their ideas in their reflection notebook.

Variation 2: Follow up the in-class part of the activity with a challenge to your students. Instruct them to spend, within the next day or so, 15 to 30 minutes in a place that is as devoid of sound as possible, especially human-produced sound. In some cases, students may have to take some initiative to create a quiet place, such as by asking their family to be extra quiet so that they can conduct this experiment at home.

Tell the students to describe afterward, in their reflection notebook, what happened during the experiment, focusing on questions such as these, which you have written on the board:

- How quiet were you able to make your place?
- Did you remain fully alert, or get drowsy or even fall asleep?
- Were you able just to "be with" the silence, or were you fidgety?
- What kind of thoughts went through your mind during this quiet time?
- Did you hear anything out of the ordinary or new? If so, what was it?
- Would you be willing to try the experience again? Would you make it a regular habit? Why or why not?

Being Pulled Apart

This activity helps students recognize that nearly everyone must deal with distractions and pressures, and we are not alone in sometimes feeling overwhelmed.

Move all the furniture and desks against the wall and divide the class into groups of three. Then give the following instructions:

- Choose one person in your triad to stand with arms stretched out to the sides at shoulder height. The other two people will each grab one wrist of the person with the outstretched arms. When I say, "Go," the two on the sides will gently pull on the arms of the person in the middle, in a friendly game of tug-of-war. Meanwhile, the person in the middle will try to move forward. Remember, we all want to keep our limbs intact, so pull gently! Okay, "Go!"

After 30 seconds, call the tugging to a halt. Have the group members take turns pulling and being pulled until each person has been in the middle position. Allow 30 seconds for each tugging time.

Facilitate a large-group discussion using questions such as the following:

- How did it feel to be tugged on while trying to move forward? to be doing the pulling?
- What can this tug-of-war exercise tell us about stress?
- What are some stresses you commonly experience that keep you from moving forward?
- How does too much stress affect your ability to reach your goals?
- What are some positive things you can do to reduce the pull of stress in your life?

Variation: If the classroom is not large enough for all the students to do the tug-of-war exercise, ask three volunteers to demonstrate in front of the class before the discussion.

7

Some Stress Can Be Good

This small-group activity helps students see that positive stress can be helpful and negative stress is destructive.

1. Divide the class into groups of about five students each. Spread the groups as far apart as possible within the room. Ask one person in each group to do the writing for the group. Instruct the designated writers to take a sheet of paper and write the alphabet down the margin on the left-hand side.

2. Tell the students their group will be competing with the other groups to complete an assigned task in 3 minutes. They are to work together within their group as effectively as possible and not consult with any members of the other groups. After these preliminary instructions, say to the groups:
   * For each letter of the alphabet, write down the word for an animal that begins with that letter. Begin now.
   Start timing as soon as you finish speaking, and stop the activity after 3 minutes. Ask all the groups to put down their pens or pencils and compare how they did in completing their task.

3. Call for feedback on the activity from the entire class, based on these or similar questions:
   * How did having a deadline affect the work of your group?
   * What kind of process did you use? Did you call out suggestions randomly? or systematically work through the alphabet?
   * How did competition with other groups affect how your group approached its task?
   * Did you experience the stress of the competition as a positive force? Why or why not?

4. Close the discussion with comments along these lines:
   * Stress can be either a positive force or a negative force. A rubber band provides an example of this: you have to stretch it and put tension on it in order to get it around things, but if you stretch it too far, it will break and no longer be useful.

      Too much stress can overwhelm us and prevent us from completing our task. Certain kinds of stress are downright destructive, even in small amounts. But sometimes stress can be helpful, such as by motivating us to work effectively and cooperatively during a friendly competition. The key is keeping things in proper perspective and finding ways to use stress to our advantage.

Variation: Before conveying the closing comments, give the groups another task. This time, assign each group a different task, and vary these tasks in difficulty from extremely easy to almost impossible. Then ask the students to compare this experience with their previous one.

Nurtured Faith

This reflective demonstration helps students see how Christian meditation can help them nurture their relationship with God.

1. Bring two plants to class—one that is obviously well cared for and healthy, and one that is obviously neglected and doing very poorly. Place the plants where everyone can see them clearly.

2. Direct the class's attention to the plants. Ask your students to spend a few minutes pondering the similarities between either of the two plants and their own relationship with God. Direct the students to write down, in their reflection notebook, which plant their faith most resembles and then list some reasons why their faith is in the condition it is.

3. After 5 to 10 minutes, pair up the students and ask them to share their responses with their partner.

4. Conclude the activity with a comment about how meditation helps us develop healthy and thriving relationships with God—much the same way a little care and attention produces healthy, thriving plants. In both cases, a bit of extra effort may be required on our part, but the results are usually well worth it.

Finding Our Balance

This demonstration and discussion builds on pages 102–103 in the student text, on how meditation can bring God back into our life and give us perspective and balance.

Ask everyone to get out of their chair and stretch. Tell the students that when you say, "Now," they are to stand on one foot as long as they can. Warn them that they may not hold on to anything or anyone for support. As soon as they touch something to regain their balance, they must sit down in their chair. Give the signal to start.

After most of the students have had to sit, conduct a discussion on the lessons this exercise teaches about meditation. Look for responses such as these:

• Sometimes we lose our balance in life and need God's support, which we can gain through meditation.
• Meditation can help us bring back (or maintain) balance in our life.
• Meditation gives us the inner strength to keep our balance.
• Without something like meditation to balance us, our life (or our faith) will be shaky and weak.

Close by comparing meditation to the pole a tightrope walker uses for balance.

Section B: Approaching Meditation

Pages 105–108 of the student text acknowledge that no one way of meditating fits everyone. Beginners benefit from letting time and experience help them find the best way—or ways—for them. As different as the meditation methods are, they do share some common features: they open our mind to the world around us and to God; require a quiet space, a regular time, and a comfortable posture; and challenge us to let go of distracting thoughts and be attentive to the present moment.

What Can Meditation Do for Me?

This home assignment and discussion asks students to look at their personal temperament and approach to prayer, and, in light of these, anticipate the benefits they will gain from practicing meditation.

Handout 7–A

Assign for homework the section "Approaching Meditation" in the student text, pages 105–108, and distribute handout 7–A, "What Can Meditation Do for Me?" Instruct your students to complete the handout after they finish their reading assignment. They should be prepared to share their responses in small groups. At the next class, form small groups of four and give the groups at least 20 minutes to share their handout responses.

Floating Away

This quick exercise gives students a chance to practice dealing in a calm, unforced way with the inevitable stray thoughts and distractions that accompany meditation.

7

1. Begin by reassuring your students that everyone who practices meditation experiences distracting thoughts that take them away from the present moment. Emphasize that the best way to deal with these thoughts is to remain calm about them and to avoid trying to force them to go away. The best response to wondering thoughts is to simply and passively let them float away.

2. Ask the students to sit up straight in their seat and to close their eyes. Then slowly say to them:
- Take a few slow, deep breaths and let all your thoughts drain out of your head as you exhale. . . . Quiet your eyes and let their gaze fall toward your lap. . . . Turn your focus inward, and let your mind just rest peacefully without thinking. . . . *[Pause for 30 seconds]*

  Any time you sense a thought wandering in, remain calm and passive and simply allow the thought to float right past you like a fluffy cloud. Then, very gently bring your attention back to your quiet downward gaze and feel the thought evaporate.

Allow the students to practice floating their thoughts away for 2 full minutes. Then tell them to slowly bring their attention back to the classroom and to open their eyes when they are ready.

3. Spend 5 minutes or so getting feedback from the students about the exercise.

Section C: Ways of Meditating

Pages 108–116 of the student text provide numerous opportunities for students to experience different ways of meditating. The first section invites students to meditate with nature, to listen to the sounds of silence, and to pay attention to their breathing and the parts of their body as a way to unwind and relax. The second section offers students ways to listen to God—through finding a tranquil setting, handing over burdens to God, and offering a centering prayer. The last section takes students step by step through a guided meditation and a reflection on that experience.

The exercises in the student text provide an excellent introduction to meditative experiences, but are difficult to read and practice at the same time. To help your students make the most of these suggestions, lead them through some or all of these exercises during class. Before assigning "Ways of Meditating" in the student text, pages 108–116, for reading, explain to your students that they will have an opportunity to do at least some of the suggested activities during class. Tell them that although they may try any of these on their own as they read, they need not feel obligated to do so.

For several of the activities, you may want to meet in a setting where the students are free to spread out and make themselves more comfortable than is possible in a classroom.

Walking Meditation

The movement of our body in walking or hiking can give a rhythm and meter to our prayer. Take your students for a walk in a park or a hike through a woods. Restrict talking so that the students will be attentive to the sounds, smells, and sights of nature and can be alone with their thoughts and prayers.

Variation 1: During the walk, allow some time for the students to go off a short distance by themselves to sit quietly and be alone in nature.

Variation 2: If a nearby retreat center has an outdoor stations of the cross, plan a meditative field trip to the site.

Variation 3: Urge the students to look for opportunities to do a walking meditation on their own.

The Lord's Prayer with Motions

This exercise for praying the Lord's Prayer without saying any words allows students to experience another way of using their body for prayer and meditation.

Practice this a few times before doing the prayer with the students. Let the students know that they will be praying the Lord's Prayer using motions instead of words. Ask them to stand and echo your motions. You might want to go through the prayer twice, the first time with you saying the words and the second time with the motions alone. Use the following modern-language version of the prayer:

- Our Father
  [Raise arms in front of body]
  Who is in heaven
  [Raise arms above head]
  Holy is your name
  [Cross arms over chest]
  Your kingdom come
  [Raise right arm in front of body]
  Your will be done
  [Raise left arm in front of body]
  On earth
  [Bring both arms down in front of body and bend at waist until almost touching floor]
  As it is in heaven
  [Stand up straight, and raise arms above head and hold them apart]
  Please give us
  [Bring arms down in front of body with palms up]
  All that we need
  [Bring cupped hands in close to body]
  And forgive us
  [Drop hands to side, drop head on chest, and droop shoulders]
  All our sins
  [Bring both hands up, fingers apart, to sides of face]
  As we forgive
  [Drop hands to side, drop head on chest, and droop shoulders]
  Those who harm us
  [Bring both hands up, fingers apart, to sides of face]
  And lead us not
  [Step forward, bring arms behind body]
  Away from you
  [Step back, raising arms in front of body]
  Amen
  [Bring folded hands to chest and bow head]

A Meditation in Your Hands

This is a variation of the palms down, palms up meditation found on pages 111–112 of the student text.

Read the following instructions to your students slowly, pausing after each line:

- Sit comfortably, close your eyes, and relax.
  Place your hands down at your side and clench your fists tightly together.
  Take a few moments to think about all the things that make you angry and bitter.
  Offer these in prayer to the Lord.
  Let go of the anger and open your hands. *[Pause longer]*
  Rest your hands gently in your lap, palms down.

Take a few moments to think of all the things that make you happy
and at ease.
Offer these in prayer to the Lord.
Thank God for the joys, and open your hands. *[Pause longer]*
Cup your hands gently in the shape of a bowl.
Take a few minutes to think of all your needs right now.
Offer these in prayer to the Lord.
Ask God to answer your needs with open hands. *[Pause longer]*
Reach your hands up to the Lord.
Take a few minutes to think of all the things you are grateful for.
Offer these in prayer to the Lord.
Praise and thank God with open hands.

Meditation Takes Practice

This at-home exercise encourages students to put into practice the basic guidelines for meditation and to experiment with the ways that work best for them.
This activity is best used toward the end of the class's work with this chapter,
after the students have had some guided practice doing several of the meditations from their text.

1. Review with your students the common features of meditation found
on pages 105–106 of the student text: openness, a quiet space, a regular time,
and a prayerful posture. Ask the students to select one or more of the meditations given in the section "Ways of Meditating" in their text, pages 108–116.
Direct them to spend some time during each of the next three days, using the
four guidelines to practice the meditation or meditations they selected.

2. After the three days have passed, instruct the class to discuss the following questions, which you have written on the board, in groups of three or
four students:

- Where did you find a quiet space to meditate? Did it help you feel more
comfortable and open to prayer?
- Which time of day was the best for you? Why?
- What posture did you find the most comfortable? Why? Did it depend
on what type of meditation you did?
- How can you deal with distractions during meditation? Brainstorm several tips.

Ask the groups to share with the entire class some of their tips for dealing
with distractions.

3. Close by encouraging the students to keep experimenting with and
practicing meditation. Compare meditating to playing a sport or developing
a musical or artistic talent: it takes time and dedication to learn the skills of
the task and to excel at it.

7

Meditation and Mass

Handout 7–B

This exercise tells students how to get more out of their liturgical experiences by applying what they have learned about meditation.

Pass out handout 7–B, "Meditation and Mass," toward the end of the class's work with this chapter on meditation. Encourage your students to try the technique described on the handout the next time they attend Mass, as a way to get more out of the experience.

On a Wing and a Prayer

This guided meditation uses the imagery of kite flying and offers students a creative way to present their prayers to God.

Rehearse this guided meditation before reading it to the students:

• Assume a comfortable prayer posture. . . . Relax. . . . Let all tension leave your body. . . . Breathe deeply in and out. . . . Feel the tension leave your feet . . . your legs. . . . Relax your stomach and chest. . . . Let the tension escape from your arms . . . from your neck. . . . Let your jaw and face relax. . . . Slow down. . . . Breathe in and out slowly. . . .

Imagine yourself sitting outside in a large meadow. It's a clear, cool day, and you can feel the breezes on your skin. . . . Out of the corner of your eye you notice something colorful attached to a small bush. . . . You walk over to see what it is. . . . It is a kite with many beautiful tails. . . . Untangling the kite from its snare, you begin to wonder what it would be like to be a kite. . . . You think, Wouldn't being a kite be a wonderful way to lift my prayers up to God?

Suddenly, you feel yourself become the kite. . . . On each tail you attach a prayer you want to lift up to God. . . . *[Pause a little longer for students to think of some prayers]*

The gentle breeze increases, and the edges of the kite lift slightly. . . . Within moments the wind effortlessly raises you off the ground. . . . One by one, your beautiful tails follow you up into a clear, blue sky. . . . You climb higher and higher, tugging at the string for more freedom . . . to fly. . . .

One at a time, you lift your prayers up to God and release them. . . . *[Pause a little longer]*

Once all your prayers are released, the wind ebbs and you slowly . . . and peacefully . . . glide back to earth. . . . *[Pause a little longer]*

When you are ready, return from the scene and open your eyes.

7

🌲 Clearing a Path to Jesus

If you have not done so already, consider including at least one retreat experience as part of your work with this course. Remember that the best place for a retreat is away from the school grounds.

Many of the exercises for this chapter on meditation—both in the student text and in this teaching manual—lend themselves to a retreat format. The following schedule for a one-day retreat provides just one option for organizing some of these exercises into a retreat.

9:00 a.m.	*Welcome and opening prayer:* "The Lord's Prayer with Motions" in this manual, page 88
9:15	*Large-group discussion:* Goals for the day
9:30	*Video and small-group discussion:* "The Hunger Without a Name" in this manual, page 81
10:00	Break
10:20	*Large-group activity and discussion:* "Being Pulled Apart" in this manual, page 83
11:00	*Introduction to meditation:* "Common Features" in the student text, pages 105–106
11:15	*Meditation warm-ups:* "The Sounds of Silence" in the student text, pages 108–109, and "Palms Down, Palms Up" in the student text, pages 111–112
12:00 m.	Lunch
12:45 p.m.	*Outdoor activity:* "Walking Meditation" in this manual, page 87
1:30	*Scriptural reading and written reflection:* John 14:1–7 ("I am the way, and the truth, and the life.")
2:00	*Closing prayer:* "On a Wing and a Prayer" in this manual, page 90

What Can Meditation Do for Me?

Complete the following sentences:

1. The five adjectives that best describe me are . . .

2. My favorite way to pray is . . .

3. One weakness of my prayer life is . . .

4. Given who I am and my approach to prayer, I will benefit from meditation because . . . (list at least five reasons)

5. Meditation will challenge me to . . .

6. One thing that makes me nervous about meditating is . . .

Meditation and Mass

Use the process described on this handout as a way to get more out of the next Mass you attend. Familiarize yourself with the process by reading over the steps several times before you attempt to do them.

1. Arrive ten minutes before the liturgy starts. Settle into an appropriate and comfortable prayer posture and concentrate on opening yourself up to God.

2. Close your eyes and imagine yourself seated in a calm, peaceful place inside your heart. Invite God into your heart and ask that you will be open to the message in the liturgy of the word and to the gift of Jesus the Christ in the Eucharist.

   Any time you find yourself being distracted by the people coming and taking their seats around you, gently travel back to your place of calm and peace.

3. During the liturgy, let your heart and your mind focus on the richness of the symbols in the eucharistic celebration. Let yourself experience that celebration as if for the first time.

4. When the Mass is over, stay for five minutes after everyone else leaves. Prayerfully reflect on the message of God's word and the experience of receiving Jesus in the Eucharist. Give thanks to God for these gifts.

Handout 7–B: Permission to reproduce this handout for classroom use is granted.

93

CHAPTER 8

Praying with the Scriptures: Nourished by the Word

Using the Text Activities

Each major section of the student text concludes with some sort of reflection activity. Carefully review these text activities before the students begin their work with this chapter, to decide the best way to use the activities. For example, some may be assigned along with the reading material, and others may be done during class, with the students working alone or in groups. Also, decide which activities are to be handed in to you and which ones are to be done in the students' reflection notebook. This preparation will help your students get the most out of the activities in their text.

Section A: The Word of God: A Banquet for the Spirit

Chapter 8 of the student text focuses on praying with the Scriptures. The opening section, pages 117–120, proposes that the Scriptures provide Christians with essential spiritual nourishment. The Bible's many different literary styles reflect the wide variety of ways the ancient Jews and early Christians experienced God's activity in their life. Even though the Scriptures are certainly inspired by God, they cannot be expected to teach historical facts. Instead, the Bible's concern is to convey religious truth.

8

Me, God, and the Scriptures

This activity invites students to reflect on how the stories told in the Scriptures have shaped their view of themselves and of God.

   1. Introduce the activity in this way:
   • Storytelling is a very important way people pass down and share their culture, values, and faith. Every culture has traditional tales that tell the story of the people and serve as a guide for living in the present.

This is the role the Bible plays in the life of Christians: it tells the story of who we are as a people and contains writings, inspired by God, to guide us in living our faith.

Many of us have heard biblical stories since we were small children, from our parents, in school, and at Mass. Even without our realizing it, the stories of the Scriptures have shaped the way we see ourselves and how we view God.

2. Ask your students to take out their reflection notebook and write a synopsis for each of their two favorite biblical stories. The first story should have a strong influence on their personal actions or character. After summarizing the story, the students should jot down an example from their life that reflects this influence. The second story should have shaped their view of God. Again, the students should write about an example from their life that reflects this view of God. For both stories, the students are to base their synopsis on their memory, rather than refer to a Bible.

3. Allow the students to share their completed synopses in small groups of five students each.

4. Close by affirming the effect the Scriptures have already had on the students' lives. Encourage the students to continue reading, reflecting on, and experiencing the Scriptures to learn more about themselves and God.

Variation: Use this activity for a home assignment. Allow your students to refer to a Bible for their synopses. Ask them to write, in addition to the synopses, a one-page essay for each story, reflecting on how the story has influenced them and shaped their view of God. Encourage them to include any new insights they may have gained in the process of reflecting on the story for this assignment.

The Scriptures as Literature

Handout 8–A

This home assignment helps students increase their familiarity with the location of the books of the Scriptures and with the variety of literary styles used in the Scriptures.

Use handout 8–A, "The Scriptures as Literature," to send your students on a search to discover biblical passages that contain different literary forms. Make sure each student has access to a Bible; provide one for those who do not have their own.

Instruct the students to complete as much of the handout as they can for the next class session. Caution them that whereas examples for some of the categories may be easy to find, they may have to search hard for others.

In the next class session, ask the students to provide examples of each style, citing the passage, reading at least part of it, and sharing the message they found there. As you go through the list, encourage the students to jot down passages found by their classmates that differ from their own.

Variation 1: Direct the students to do this search of the Scriptures in class, working in small groups.

Variation 2: Instead of using handout 8–A, prepare your own handout that lists certain themes, such as forgiveness, anger, praise, wonder, fear, petition, instruction, celebration, and so forth. Ask the students to search the Scriptures individually for passages reflecting those themes, or divide the class into groups and ask each group to choose a different theme from the list. In addition to a Bible, students may need to use a biblical concordance for this theme search.

A Reflection of Culture

This activity encourages students to see that although the Bible reflects the historical period, culture, and beliefs of the people who wrote it, the truths of the Bible are still fresh and relevant to us today.

1. Introduce the activity by saying something about how, in his teachings, Jesus used real-life examples that the people he was addressing could understand and identify with. Many of his followers were poor and working-class people who earned their livelihood from fishing or farming. Thus Jesus referred to lost sheep, bread baking, fishers of men, and so forth.

2. Brainstorm with the class about what examples Jesus might use if he were to address his teachings to people in their community today. Write the students' ideas on the board and continue until the class has generated at least fifteen ideas.

3. Pair up the students and assign one of the following stories to each pair:
- Matthew 20:1–16 (The laborers in the vineyard)
- Matthew 22:1–14 (The wedding banquet)
- Matthew 25:14–30 (The parable of the silver pieces)
- Mark 4:1–20 (The parable of the seed)
- Mark 4:30–34 (The mustard seed)
- Luke 11:33–36 (The parable of the lamp)
- Luke 14:7–11 (A lesson in humility)
- Luke 15:8–10 (The parable of divine mercy)
- Luke 16:19–31 (The rich man and Lazarus)
- Luke 21:1–4 (The widow's mite)
- John 8:1–11 (The adulteress)
- John 10:6–18 (The good shepherd)

Instruct the pairs to read the passage and to then rewrite it as a contemporary story, using one of the examples from the brainstormed list in step 2 of this activity or an idea of their own. Their rewritten story should be at least one page long.

4. Give the pairs until the next class session, or longer, to complete their story. Then spend time during the designated class allowing the pairs to share their story with the whole group.

8

Section B:
Come to the Feast: Prayerful Reading

This section of chapter 8 in the student text, pages 121–123, invites students to consider reading the Scriptures as a form of prayer. It presents a process to guide students in praying the Scriptures. An example shows them how they might use the process.

Scripture Response

This journal-writing exercise stresses that reading the Scriptures is an active process that calls us to respond. It lets students practice a different way of reading the Scriptures prayerfully than the process given in their text.

Write the following list of scriptural passages on the board and randomly assign each student a passage. Tell the students they will be doing a written reflection on their passage in their reflection notebook.

- 1 Corinthians 13:4–7
- John 14:15–21
- Matthew 5:1–12
- Matthew 11:28–30
- Luke 1:46–55

Pass along to the students the following instructions:

- First, read the entire passage and quietly reflect on it for a few minutes.
    Then, write out the first verse, reflect on it, and write a response to it. Write the first thing or feeling that comes into your mind. Do not worry about grammar or spelling. Next, write the second verse, reflect on it, and write your response. Repeat this pattern until you have responded to all the verses of your passage.
    Last, read and reflect on the entire passage again, and review your written responses.

Encourage the students to use this same process on their own with the other passages listed on the board. They may also choose their own passage for a verse-by-verse reflection.

Favorite Passages

This discussion lets students share with one another their favorite scriptural passage and at the same time shows them that such group sharing can be a form of prayer.

1. Ask your students to identify their favorite passage from the Scriptures and to mark the location of the passage in their Bible. Instruct the students to read their passage over before the next class and to reflect on what the passage means to them.

8

2. At the next class, form small groups of five to six students each. Explain that each student is to read his or her favorite passage to the group and share with the group the following information:

why this passage is the student's favorite

how God is speaking to the student through this passage

an example of how the student responds to this message in his or her daily life

Close by informing the students that the kind of sharing they just did is another way of praying the Scriptures.

Variation: Tell the students about any Bible study groups sponsored in their school, in their parish, or as a component of area youth groups.

Prayerful Symbols

Handout 8–B

This written exercise allows students to explore some of the symbols the gospel writer John uses to describe Jesus.

Give each student a copy of handout 8–B, "Prayerful Symbols," and ask the students to complete the handout quietly on their own. After about 20 minutes, invite the students to share their responses in a large-group discussion.

Answers to handout questions: Here is a list of the passages from the handout and their corresponding symbols for Jesus:

Passage	Symbol
John 1:29–31	Lamb of God
John 6:25–40	Bread of life
John 8:12	Light of the world
John 10:7–16	Good shepherd
John 15:1–5	True vine

Artistic Reflections

This activity allows students the freedom to express the meaning of the Scriptures through simple artistic mediums.

1. Form small groups of about six to eight students each. Explain to the groups that words are only one way we can share the meaning of the Scriptures. We can pray the Scriptures with one another through artistic means as well.

2. Write the following scriptural passages on the board and assign each group one of them:
- Matthew 5:14–16
- Luke 12:22–31
- Matthew 22:36–40
- Mark 9:33–37

Instruct the groups to have one person read the passage aloud to the others and to then spend a few moments reflecting together upon the meaning of the passage.

8

3. Ask the groups to decide between two avenues of artistic expression that they will use to share their interpretation of the passage with the rest of the class:

- *Human sculpture:* Using only the people in the group as props, the group will create a silent human sculpture representing the meaning of its scriptural passage.
- *Clay sculpture:* Using a nonmessy clay like Play-Doh, the group will create a representation of the meaning of its scriptural passage. The group will present this to the rest of the class without speaking.

  Allow about 20 minutes for the groups to create their work of art.

4. When each group presents its artistic reflection to the rest of the class, have the other students study the sculpture for a few minutes. Then ask them for any insights as to the message of the sculpture. Keep prompting the class until their insights roughly match the message from the scriptural passage the sculpture represents.

Variation: Cover a table with a wide variety of art supplies, such as crayons, markers, paint, clay, charcoal pens, pencils, paper, construction paper, glue, scissors, yarn, and magazines. Allow the students to choose from these mediums as an option in step 3 of the main activity.

Section C:
Pouring Out Your Soul: The Psalms

Pages 124–129 in the student text discuss how, through the scriptural psalms, the ancient Jews shared their deepest emotions, both positive and negative, with their God. Students are invited to expand their understanding of the psalms and to translate the psalms into their own experiences.

Verse by Verse

This before-class prayer helps students become more familiar with praying the scriptural psalms, especially the psalms of praise.

Each day that the class works with pages 124–129 of the student text, pray together praise psalm 8, 34, 47, 66, or 106. For the longer psalms, ask one student to read the first verse or two, a second student to read the second verse or two, and so on. For the shorter psalms, where you have more students in the class than the psalm has verses, ask groups of students to read the verses in turn. Make sure all the students use the same version of the Bible for this reading. Have them share Bibles if necessary.

Songs for Every Need

This small-group activity lets students discover some of the types of themes found in the scriptural psalms and to become more familiar with reading the psalms prayerfully.

Assign each student a working partner and divide all 150 psalms among the pairs. Each pair should have about 10 to 15 psalms to work with. Give a copy of handout 8–C, "Songs for Every Need," to each pair and tell the pairs to work together to complete the handout.

Handout 8–C

Variation: Follow up the handout work with a large-group discussion. Ask the class for several examples of psalms from each theme type. Have the respondents identify each psalm and then read four or five verses that express the theme.

A Different Beat

This activity helps students realize that although the scriptural psalms were written in the style and context of the ancient Jewish people, they express emotions that transcend time and place.

Form small groups of about six students each. Ask each group to choose one of the following psalms: 10, 28, 53, 109, or 142. Invite each group to translate five verses of its psalm into a contemporary music style. Offer the groups some possible music styles to choose from, such as rock, country, reggae, rap, hip-hop, heavy metal, jazz, pop, rhythm and blues, gospel, punk, alternative, or soul.

The students may either read or perform their example for the rest of the class. Advise the groups to read aloud to the class the original verses before sharing their contemporary version.

Expressing Every Emotion

This written reflection exercise stresses the importance of expressing our emotions, especially in our conversations with God. It shows students that the scriptural psalms can serve as a vehicle for emotional release and as a starting point for writing their own psalms.

1. Offer these reflections before giving your students their assignment:
• As you read in your text, the psalms are a collection of songs expressing all sorts of deep emotions that range from joy and thanks to despair and anger.

  In much of modern society, people often cover up or bury their emotions. Many consider the sharing of emotions, especially strong ones, to be inappropriate. In actuality, the ability to share feelings is a healthy thing. Emotions, even positive ones, can be kept inside for only so long before some sort of damage occurs, either to ourselves or to the people around us.

  Praying the psalms is a great way to express our emotions. These songs teach us that it is okay to share with God what we are truly feeling, even if that emotion is anger or doubt.

  The scriptural psalms can also help us express our feelings to God, by inspiring us to write psalms about our own experiences.

2. Ask the students to listen as you read a psalm written by another young person:

- **A Lamentation**
  Oh, God, do you hear me calling
  in the darkest part of night?
  I look to you for guidance
  but cannot feel your presence.
  Oh, help me to overcome this hell
  that I am living.

  I sit and cry in confusion.
  What have I done to deserve this?
  Is it what I have done
  or what I have not done?
  Oh, God, please help me to find
  the cure for evil in my world.

  Even if I see just a light in the distance,
  to know you are there,
  I will feel motivation to continue my journey.
  Give me the strength to travel my path,
  but, God, don't make me walk alone . . .
  for I am a heart with loving intentions.

  [Jennifer Filkins, in Carl Koch, editor, *Dreams Alive,* p. 12]

3. Invite the students to take a few moments to reflect on a feeling they would like to express to God right now, something they are holding in their heart and they really need to get out. Then, ask the students to take out their reflection notebook and begin writing their own psalm.

Variation: To allow for a greater sense of freedom of expression, let students do their reflection and writing at home instead of in class.

Section D:
Using Your Imagination: Stories and Parables

This section of chapter 8 in the student text, pages 130–136, invites students to use their imagination to dive inside and experience the power of scriptural stories. Two ways to do this are to find our own place in each story and to retell a parable from our own experience.

Getting in Character

This journal-writing exercise is a variation of the imagining activity suggested in the student text, on pages 131–133. It invites students to place themselves in a parable and reflect on the similarities between one of the characters and themselves.

Make comments like these to your students to introduce this exercise:
- Different parables speak to us in different ways at different times. That is the beauty of the Scriptures. Even though we may have heard a passage several times before, it may hold new meaning for us when we hear it again at a different place along our life's journey.

Tell the students to read the parable of the prodigal son in Luke 15:11–32. Instruct them to identify all the characters in the story (these are the prodigal son, the father, the older brother, the older brother's friends, the father's servants, the pigs, and the fatted calf). Ask them to write, in their reflection notebook, about the character they can relate to most and why.

Variation: Instead of telling your students to read the parable of the prodigal son, brainstorm with them a list of characters from the parables or other stories in the Scriptures, and write this list on the board. Let the students choose their character for this exercise from the list. Suggest that the students use a concordance to look up their character in a Bible, in order to refresh their memory of the situation and to stimulate their reflection.

Parable Witness

This witness talk uses peer ministry to help students make the connection between a parable story and their own experience.

Invite a student from another class or grade to give a witness talk to your class, preferably someone who has given such a talk before, as at a retreat.

Handout 8–D

Give the witnessing student a copy of handout 8–D, "Witness Talk on the Parable of the Lost Sheep," and enough time to prepare. Offer to hear the talk beforehand and give feedback.

Prepare the class by explaining that a witness talk is a chance for sharing personal faith and requires their attentiveness and respect.

Allow some time for questions or dialog between the class and the speaker after the talk, followed by some quiet time for written reflection.

Scripture in the News

This essay assignment helps students recognize that lessons from the parables can be applied to real situations in our community and nation.

As a home assignment, tell your students to find a story from a newspaper, a news magazine, the radio, or television, with a parallel to a story from the Scriptures. Give the students a week to find their news story and to write a two-page essay on how the scriptural story relates to the news story, particularly in terms of the themes, the characters, and the lessons to be learned.

If your schedule permits, allow the students to present their essays to one another in small groups.

Live, from the Gospels

This drama activity invites students to retell scriptural stories using the contemporary format of broadcast media.

Form small groups of about six to eight students each. Assign each group one of the Gospel stories listed on pages 133 and 136 of the student text.

Give these instructions to the groups:

- Imagine you are a TV news crew that has just arrived at the scene of a breaking scriptural story. You need to decide how you are going to give a live, two-minute report on this event for the evening news broadcast.

  Decide among yourselves who in the group will be anchors, reporters, and camera operators, as well as some of the characters in the story. You have twenty minutes to prepare your story before you go on the air.

After 20 minutes, let the groups "air" their broadcast for the entire class.

Variation 1: If video equipment is available at your school, or you or a student can bring a recorder from home, videotape the broadcasts and air them on a classroom television.

Variation 2: Suggest to your students that they translate their story into a contemporary setting before broadcasting the event.

Fireworks

This prayer service uses music, responsive reading, and reflection to show how the Scriptures can be a continuous source of surprise and excitement in our relationship with God. It also invites students to reflect on the miracles in the Scriptures and the miracles that occur in their everyday life.

Use this prayer service to conclude the class's work on praying with the Scriptures.

Preparation

Handout 8–E

1. Several days before the prayer service is held, make enough copies of handout 8–E, "Go Out to All the World," for everyone in the class.

2. Collect a tape player or CD player and the tape or CD *River of Souls*, by Dan Fogelberg (Epic cassette tape ET-46934 or Epic compact disk EK-46934, September 1993), and copies of the songbook *Glory and Praise*, classic edition.

3. Gather a slide projector and a dozen or more slides of fireworks. Sort through the slides and match an appropriate one with each of the scriptural passages on handout 8–E. Also choose an ending slide, to show after the last scriptural reading and response. You will need a total of twelve slides for the presentation.

4. Ask several students to create a colorful banner of fireworks by using colored chalk on black construction paper. Hang the banner in the center of the space you will be using for prayer.

5. Choose eleven students to read for the Scripture-slide presentation. Give each reader a copy of handout 8–E and assign each reader one of the scriptural passages on the handout. Ask the readers to look up their passage in their Bible and review it several times before the prayer service.

8

Procedure

1. Begin the prayer service by playing the song "Magic Every Moment," by Dan Fogelberg, from the tape or CD *River of Souls*. Then offer this call to prayer:

- In the song you just heard, the singer discovers a miracle when an injured dove recovers and is able to fly. This miracle makes him reflect and thank God for the people who are miracles in his life. He starts to recognize that it is easy to miss these miracles, to take them for granted, because we get caught up in day-to-day living.

   Let's try to be sensitive to the moments when God is revealed to us. The Scriptures can be a source of surprise and wonder if we open ourselves up to the magic of God's love.

2. Distribute copies of handout 8–E to the rest of the class. Ask everyone to join in the response after each scriptural reading.

Dim the lights so that everyone can see the slides well but still read their materials. Then project the first slide on the screen and signal the first reader to begin.

Pause briefly after each group response, and then move to the next fireworks slide and next reading.

3. While still showing the last slide, pause for a few moments of quiet. Proceed with this oral reflection on fireworks and the Scriptures:

- The Scriptures are a lot like fireworks.

   They explode and spread across the distance of time and the barriers of language and culture. They burst forth again and again with new meaning. Sometimes the revelation comes as a surprise.

   No two scriptural passages are alike. Each has a special message for us, inspired by God.

   The Scriptures delight and excite. We often take them for granted, but they are a dramatic, astounding way that God speaks to us.

   No one watches fireworks alone. They are part of a community celebration. May all of us, as sisters and brothers in Christ, continually celebrate and experience the power of the Scriptures.

   Let us give thanks to God for the miracle of the word given to us in the Scriptures.

   Amen.

4. Bring the lights back to normal and shut off the slide projector. Close by singing the song "What You Hear in the Dark," by Dan Schutte, in *Glory and Praise,* classic edition.

8

The Scriptures as Literature

Search through the Hebrew Scriptures and the Christian Testament to find an example of each of the following literary styles. Record the exact location of the example, and summarize its main message.

Style	Citation	Message
Story	_____	_____
Legend	_____	_____
Myth	_____	_____
History	_____	_____
Conversation	_____	_____
Letter	_____	_____
List	_____	_____
Biography	_____	_____
Law	_____	_____
Speech	_____	_____
Poem	_____	_____
Parable	_____	_____
Proverb	_____	_____
Advice	_____	_____
Wise teaching	_____	_____
Song	_____	_____
Prayer	_____	_____

Prayerful Symbols

In each passage listed here, the Gospel writer John uses a symbol to teach readers something important about Jesus. For each passage, read the verse or verses in your Bible, write down the symbol used for Jesus, and answer these two questions:

1. What does this symbol teach us about Jesus?
2. How can this symbol help us relate to Jesus?

John 1:29–31

John 6:25–40

John 8:12

John 10:7–16

John 15:1–5

Handout 8–B: Permission to reproduce this handout for classroom use is granted.

Songs for Every Need

From your assigned list, identify the psalms that reflect each of the following types of themes. Note that some psalms contain only one theme type, whereas others express several.

Praise Psalms (Giving Glory to God)

Wisdom Psalms (Offering a Guide for Human Conduct)

Royal Psalms (Asking God's Guidance for the King)

Thanksgiving Psalms (Expressing Gratitude for Blessings)

Lamentation Psalms (Crying Out in Woe and Misfortune)

Handout 8–C: Permission to reproduce this handout for classroom use is granted.

107

Witness Talk on the Parable of the Lost Sheep

Prepare a witness talk centering around the parable of the lost sheep, Luke 15:1–7. Read or creatively retell the parable at some point in your talk, probably the beginning.

Reflect on the following questions and directives as you prepare your witness talk. Feel free to structure and shape your talk as you see fit. In other words, it is not at all necessary for your talk to follow the order of these questions and directives.

- At baptism we were accepted into the Christian community. How does the Good Shepherd continue to call us to be part of the flock? Is it possible to be lost within the flock?
- What are some ways people get lost today? (For example, through drugs, alcohol, video games, overwork.)
- Describe a time when you felt lost.
- Contrast the feelings of acceptance and rejection.
- Identify people who have helped you feel that you belong.
- Why is a sense of belonging important to your self-worth?
- How can you keep others from feeling left out? How can you invite them to be part of our community of Christians?
- How can you help others experience Jesus, the good shepherd?
- Identify the feelings associated with these activities in the parable: losing, seeking, finding, rejoicing.
- How do the symbols in the parable of the lost sheep speak to you?

General Guidelines

Here are some general guidelines for preparing and giving a witness talk:
- Share your feelings; be open and honest.
- Share examples and stories from your own life.
- Speak slowly and thoughtfully.
- Prepare an outline of your talk, but do not read word for word.
- Practice giving the talk to someone, and ask for feedback.
- Try to keep eye contact with your listeners.
- Use a scriptural passage, song, or poem to help make your point.
- Try to keep your talk to fifteen to twenty minutes.
- End with a challenge or something for listeners to think about.
- Most important, be yourself.

Go Out to All the World

Reader 1: Luke 2:1–12
All: Go out to all the world and tell the Good News.

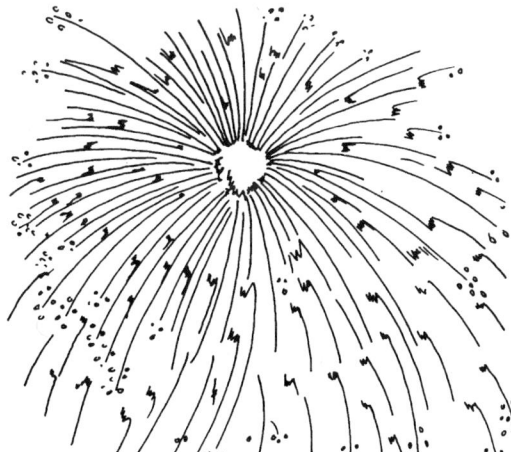

Reader 2: John 4:6–9
All: Go out to all the world and tell the Good News.

Reader 3: John 2:1–5
All: Go out to all the world and tell the Good News.

Reader 4: John 9:6–7
All: Go out to all the world and tell the Good News.

Reader 5: Mark 8:6–9
All: Go out to all the world and tell the Good News.

Reader 6: Luke 4:40–41
All: Go out to all the world and tell the Good News.

Reader 7: Matthew 9:20–22
All: Go out to all the world and tell the Good News.

Reader 8: John 11:39–44
All: Go out to all the world and tell the Good News.

Reader 9: Luke 17:12–14
All: Go out to all the world and tell the Good News.

Reader 10: Mark 14:22–24
All: Go out to all the world and tell the Good News.

Reader 11: Matthew 28:5–10
All: Go out to all the world and tell the Good News.

CHAPTER 9

Community Prayer:
Binding Us Together with God

Section A:
Community Rituals: United in Words and Actions

The opening section of chapter 9 in the student text, pages 137–143, places community prayer within the context of the universal human needs for community and ritual. All rituals build up community. When prayer is added to community rituals, an even stronger bond is created, one reinforced by God. The community at prayer gathers to seek God's help, to give praise and thanks, to seek and offer forgiveness, and to mark special occasions.

C-O-M-M-U-N-I-T-Y

This activity illustrates the value of each individual's contributions to a community.

1. Before class, spell out the word C-O-M-M-U-N-I-T-Y on nine large index cards—one letter on each card—using an extralarge marker. Remove the card with the letter *U* and set it aside where your students will not be able to see it. Scramble the remaining letter cards.

2. To begin the activity in class, give eight students each a letter card, keeping the *U* card hidden. Ask the volunteers to stand in a row in front of the class so that the rest of the students can see their letters. Then instruct the volunteers to form a word using the letter cards they are holding. If they have difficulty, invite the rest of the class to assist. At some point the students will figure out what the word is and ask for the missing letter; give it to them so that they can complete the word.

3. Thank the volunteers and ask them to return to their seat. Lead a large-group discussion based on this question:
  • What does this exercise teach us about the nature of community?
  Look for answers similar to these:
• The community is incomplete if you are missing from it.
• Each person has a role to play in the community.

9

- The community is stronger when all support it.
- A community works together to solve problems.

4. Close this activity by reiterating in your own words a number of points from the student text:
  - All of us are part of many communities, both large and small.
  - Each of us is strengthened by being part of these communities.
  - Our membership gives strength to these communities.
  - Even though we are diverse in our interests, gifts, and talents, many things bind us together.

Variation: Spell out the name of your school instead of the word *community.* Remove a key letter and use the rest of the activity as given, with emphasis on building up your school community.

Beauty in Diversity

This activity shows students that community does not mean sameness, that a healthy community can be diverse while still working toward a mutual goal.

1. Prepare for this activity by purchasing an eight-can set of Play-Doh—each can a different color.

2. Begin the activity by giving each student a piece of Play-Doh about the size of a half-dollar. Make sure that at least two people have each color of Play-Doh. Instruct the students to work with their piece of Play-Doh to see what they can create from it.

3. After 2 to 3 minutes, tell the students to get together with the other students who have the same color of Play-Doh as they do and see what they can create as a group. Let the groups work together for another 2 to 3 minutes.

4. Combine color groups—for example, blues and reds, greens and yellows, and so forth—and have each group work together on one creation. Continue until the entire class is combined into one group working to make one creation.

5. Draw this exercise to a conclusion with comments such as the following:
  - Each of you started out with a small piece of Play-Doh, which represented you as an individual and the gifts and talents you possess. As you grouped together your Play-Doh and your gifts, the possibilities of what you could do with your Play-Doh increased. Finally, when you all came together, you were able to create something no one of you could have produced on your own.

    When you become part of a community, you do not lose your individuality. Who you are might grow and change, but you are always you. In the exercise we just did, your final large clay creation is not one color, but many. Now that all these colors are bound together, it would be difficult to break them down into the individual pieces you started with. Nevertheless, you can see the separate colors when you look at the whole. The best communities are those that draw strength and beauty from diversity, and that seek to maintain that diversity even in the midst of unity.

9

My Favorite Celebration

This activity invites students to share their favorite celebration with one another and to examine the meaning of the words, actions, and symbols of a ritual associated with this occasion.

As a home assignment, pass out handout 9–A, "My Favorite Celebration," and request that your students fill it out in preparation for a small-group sharing in the next class session. Invite the students to bring any personal photographs or small items that will help them describe the occasion and its ritual to their classmates.

At the next class session, form small groups of four students each and allow about 20 minutes for sharing.

Rituals from Other Cultures

This home assignment asks students to research rituals found in other cultures and highlights their text's point that the need for ritual is universally human.

Give your students a week to identify a ritual not commonly found in their culture and to write a two-page report on that ritual. Instruct them to describe the ritual in some detail, answering these questions:
- What event does it celebrate?
- Who participates in it?
- What are its key words, actions, and symbols?
- In what ways does it help build community for the culture?

Recommend possible sources of information that can be found in most libraries, such as *National Geographic* magazine.

Variation 1: If applicable, encourage your students to compare the ritual they researched and the event it celebrates with a similar event in their own culture.

Variation 2: If your students come from diverse cultural backgrounds, allow them to write a report on the traditions that are part of their family's ritual celebrations. Lead a large-group discussion in which students compare and contrast these traditions.

Building Community

This group prayer activity identifies how both the gifts of individuals and gathering in prayer build up community. It also shows that a community that celebrates together through prayer supports all its members.

1. At the end of the first day that the class works with community rituals, provide each student with a list of all the students in this prayer course. Each student should also receive one index card for every two students in the class—if the class has thirty students, then each student needs fifteen index cards.

2. Give the students these two home assignments:
- Instruct the students to cut their index cards in half. On one side of each half, they are to write the name of a person in the class, and on the other side, they are to write one way that person is a gift to the community of this

prayer course or to their school community in general. (Emphasize the importance of taking this seriously and writing positive comments only.) When the students have filled out a card for everyone in the class, they are to bind together their cards with a rubber band.

• Tell the students to cover the lid and the bottom of a shoe box with wrapping paper (or any other kind of paper), being sure the lid can still be lifted off the box. (You may want to have a wrapped box to show your students what you mean.) They are then to write their name in large, readable letters on the top of the box lid.

Give the students two or three days to complete these assignments. Request that they bring their completed index cards and boxes to class on a specific day.

3. On the assigned day, collect the boxes and index cards from the students. After class, put each index card in the box marked with the same student's name. Put the boxes away in a secure cupboard or closet to make sure no one has access to them.

4. On the last day that the class works with this section on community rituals, bring out the boxes and invite the students to take part in a community "build-up" prayer. The students will each take someone else's box—not her or his own—and all will sit in a circle for prayer. One at a time, they will announce whose box they have, pull from the box three affirmation messages about that person, and read the messages to the class. After they put the messages back in the box, they will place the box in the center of the circle.

Before moving on to the next person, everyone will pray, "Lord, thank you for the gift of *[name of person just affirmed]*," and the entire group will applaud.

5. Offer this closing prayer after everyone in the class has been affirmed:

• Each person is a gift. Through our affirmations we have supported and built up the people gathered in our midst. As we shared these affirmations in prayer, we built up the community of our class and strengthened our bond to the community of Christ's followers. Let us continue to build up our community with our kind words and actions and through our shared prayer. Amen.

Make sure the students collect their box and encourage everyone to take some time that evening to read all the messages in their box.

Prayer Starters

The following four prayer starters can be used with "Occasions for Communal Prayer" in the student text, pages 142–143.

Asking God's Help

At the start of class, invite your students to offer a prayer of petition for friends and relatives who are experiencing some sort of difficulty.

Praising and Thanking God

Offer each student a fold-over thank-you card. Ask the students to write a prayer of praise and thanksgiving to God for all the many blessings in their life. After 3 to 5 minutes, invite everyone to read their thank-you note prayerfully in silence. Urge the students to tape their note onto a page in their reflection notebook.

Reconciling

Brainstorm with your students a list of world situations, in which healing and reconciliation are needed. Invite the students to sing the song "Peace Prayer," by John Foley, in the classic edition of *Glory and Praise,* as a prayer asking God to bring peace to the world.

Special Occasions

Encourage your students to attend a special prayer occasion for an individual, family, or parish community—such as a baptism. Suggest that they record in their reflection notebook their feelings about and reactions to being part of the celebration.

Section B:
Creating Community Prayers and Rituals

The major portion of this chapter in the student text, the section on pages 143–152, takes students through the practical steps in creating a meaningful community prayer experience. The text explains that this process begins with selecting a theme and creating an appropriate environment. Next, the environment, readings, symbols, music, and shared prayer must be woven together in a manner that involves and touches those gathered for prayer.

Using the Text Activities

As in some of the previous chapters of the student text, the section "Creating Community Prayers and Rituals" gives students specific activities to do as they read their text. Your students will get the most out of this material if you plan ahead.

The suggestions in this section of the teaching manual are meant to help you in your planning. The first activity offers a comprehensive way of dealing with this section of the student text. The other activities correspond with the specific steps for planning a prayer service outlined in the student text. For each step, consider doing the activity suggested in this teaching manual as a warm-up, before your students do the text activity for the step.

The Real Thing

This exercise gives students a specific context within which to practice the steps discussed in their text.

Let the students work in pairs or groups of three to plan a prayer service for a real community. Ask each pair or triad to choose its own community. Assist the students by recommending the following communities, or others. Encourage as much variety among the class as possible.
- the students of this prayer course
- the whole school
- your youth group

- your local parish
- a club or sports team you belong to
- your whole grade (for example, all seniors)
- your family
- an individual who is ill, and her or his family

Once the pairs or triads have selected their community, tell them to use the steps given in their text as a guide for creating their prayer service. They should answer all questions posed by the text with their chosen community in mind.

After the pairs or triads have gone through all the planning steps, have them hand in a copy of an outline of their complete prayer service.

For extra credit, encourage your students actually to hold their prayer service for their group by the end of the prayer course. Require them to turn in a one-page evaluation of how their prayer service went, including what they would do differently.

From Topic to Theme

Handout 9–B

This exercise allows students to practice picking prayer service topics and then narrowing down the topics to specific, manageable themes.

Give each student a copy of handout 9–B, "From Topic to Theme," after reviewing pages 144–145 in the student text, on choosing a topic and a theme. Instruct each student to complete only part A for each segment of the handout.

When the students have completed the A parts, tell them to exchange handouts with another student and complete part B for each segment of the handout.

Collect the handouts. Randomly select and read aloud several topics and their corresponding theme. Ask the class to evaluate each topic and how well the given theme matches it.

Keep these handouts for future reference.

What's Wrong with This Picture?

This activity is a fun way to emphasize how the right or wrong environment can make or break a prayer service.

Preparation

1. Gather some Halloween decorations; a copy of an Advent wreath blessing or other Christmas prayer; a tape player or CD player and a tape or CD of an instrumental version of your country's national anthem; a large Easter basket; and for each student in the class, one colored plastic egg that pulls apart.

2. Write about ten nonsensical prayers of petition on slips of paper and place them in some of the eggs. Fill the remaining eggs with blank slips of paper.

3. Before the students enter, prepare the classroom by doing the following:
- Put up the Halloween decorations throughout the room.
- Remove some of the desks or chairs so that several people will not have a place to sit.
- Put a plastic egg on the seat of each remaining desk and place the basket in a back corner of the room where it is difficult to see.

9

- Write the Christmas prayer on the board in letters so small that only the students in the front row will be able to read it.
- Set up the tape player or CD player and have the tape or CD ready to play. Set the volume so that the national anthem is just slightly louder than would be appropriate for background music.

Procedure

1. When the students enter the room, do not make any attempt to find seats for those without them. If someone sits on their egg and breaks it, do not offer them a new one.

2. Turn on the national anthem and invite your students to begin class with prayer. Ask them to read aloud the Christmas prayer on the board.

3. Randomly call on several students to read the prayer of petition contained in their Easter egg, and to put it in the basket at the back of the room when they are done.

4. Stop this exercise after the third or fourth egg prayer, and conduct a large-group discussion focused on these questions:
- What was wrong with this prayer service?
- How does a poorly planned environment distract from prayer?
- Based on what was wrong with this prayer service, what are some key things to look for in creating a good prayer environment?
- Why is environment an important part of a prayer service?
- If you were planning an Advent prayer service, how would you set up the environment?

The Right Reading

This exercise teaches students how to look for readings that reflect the theme of their prayer service.

Preparation

1. Bring to class several copies of each of the following reference resources: a biblical commentary, a biblical concordance, a dictionary of the Bible, and a lectionary.

2. Choose a topic and theme that go with the liturgical season of the year you are closest to while working on this section of the chapter. Write the topic and theme on the board.

Procedure

1. With the whole class, explain how to use each of the scriptural resources you have available. Then divide the students into groups of four and distribute the resources among the groups.

2. Ask the students to find at least two passages—one from the Hebrew Scriptures and one from the Christian Testament—that go with the topic and theme on the board.

9

3. Instruct each group to brainstorm some poems, lyrics, stories, or other nonbiblical readings that might also go with the topic and theme.

4. Call the class back together in a large group. Invite each foursome to share what it came up with, reading a few verses of its scriptural passages and describing the other readings it would use.

Variation: Allow the foursomes to choose their own topic and theme for this exercise.

Symbols and Symbolic Actions

This activity allows students to focus on the symbol part of a prayer service and to get feedback on their thoughts. If your students are working in pairs or triads to create a prayer service for a real community, as suggested in the activity "The Real Thing" in this manual, pages 114–115, allow them time in class to come up with some possible symbols and symbolic actions. Circulate among the groups, listening to their ideas and making suggestions if they are stumped.

Variation: Invite each working group to present its ideas to the rest of the class for comments and evaluation. Suggest that the group first tell the class what its topic and theme are and give a brief synopsis of the readings it has chosen.

Mood Music

This activity offers students experience in judging the appropriateness of music for prayer services, by asking them to evaluate the music used in rituals in which they regularly participate.

Handout 9–C

Distribute handout 9–C, "Music Evaluation." Ask your students to complete the handout after the next community prayer experience they participate in—for most, this will be the upcoming Sunday Mass.

Variation 1: Encourage your students to attend additional services at other area churches—both Catholic and non-Catholic—in order to experience the music of their rituals. Make extra copies of handout 9–C for them to use at these services.

Variation 2: Instead of directing your students to attend upcoming prayer services, ask them to think about some memorable prayer services or rituals they attended in the past and to recall the music used at them. Instruct the students to write a short essay for one such service in which they thought the music was good, and another short essay for a service in which they thought the music was bad.

For each essay, the students should give some background on the service or ritual—what, where, and when—and at least three reasons for their evaluation of the music. Offer the students handout 9–C as a guide for their evaluation.

9

Shared Prayer

This activity offers some additional possibilities for including shared prayer in prayer services. Either practice some of the following ideas with your students or offer the list to your students for use in developing their prayer service:

- Light one large pillar candle and turn off all the lights in the prayer space. Pass the candle around the group, asking each person to offer a prayer to Jesus, thanking him for lighting up their life.
- Ask each participant to write a petition on a slip of paper, and collect the petitions in a bag. Pass the bag around the circle. Direct each person in turn to pull out a prayer and read it to the group.
- Gather the participants into a circle. Pass a red rose around the circle and ask each person to say a prayer for someone whose life is endangered—who has not yet been born, who is handicapped, who is elderly and ill, and so forth.
- Before the prayer service, obtain from your local parish office a list of names and addresses of persons in the community who are not able to leave their home or take part in community activities because of age or illness. At the service, distribute the list to the participants. Ask them to pick someone from the list and to send a postcard prayer to that person. Make sure everyone on the list will receive a postcard.
- Give each person a piece of a jigsaw puzzle and invite the participants to offer a prayer asking God to help them find the missing piece in their life.
- Before the prayer service, ask the participants to bring in a snapshot of their family. During shared prayer, invite them to offer a prayer of thanks for their family, and then post their picture on a poster board "Wall of Honor."
- Before a prayer service with one or more graduating seniors present, gather pushpins and a large map. At the service, invite the seniors to come forward and place a pin on the map at the location where they will be going after graduation. After each person places his or her pin, lead the others in offering this prayer: "We pray for your success and happiness in the days and years to come."

Variation: Refer to several of the topics and themes from handout 9–B, "From Topic to Theme," if your students completed it, or generate some topics and themes on your own. Help the class brainstorm creative ideas for shared prayers on these topics and themes.

Starting in Different Places

9

This activity invites students to think of creative ways of structuring their prayer service.

Request that your students bring to class a rough outline of the prayer service they have been developing. Join each pair or triad with another group. Instruct the students to help one another come up with a prayer service structure that differs from the standard format suggested on pages 151–152 of their text.

Reassure the working groups that they are free to decide on a different final format for their prayer service—that they do not have to follow the format that emerges from this activity.

My Favorite Celebration

Reflect on all the celebrations you have been a part of or witnessed, and choose your favorite. Feel free to think of celebrations in as wide a sense as you want. They may be as elaborate and organized as a wedding, or as simple as a special picnic with your family. They may be a one-time occasion, such as the baptism of a sibling, or an annual occasion, such as a Christmas pageant. They may be as nonpersonal as the opening ceremonies of the Olympics, or as personal as your sixteenth birthday party.

Once you have decided on your favorite celebration, respond to the following directives and questions:

1. Briefly describe your favorite celebration and give some reasons why it is your favorite.

2. Pick one ritual associated with your favorite celebration and answer these questions about some of its main details:

   a. What particular words or sayings are part of the ritual? Why?

   b. What actions are part of the ritual? Why?

   c. What symbols are key to the ritual? What do the symbols stand for?

3. Summarize what your celebration would be like without this ritual.

From Topic to Theme

Seasons of the Year

Part A

Identify two topics that relate to the seasons of the year.

Topic 1: _____

Topic 2: _____

Part B

Write a theme that goes with each topic from part A.

Theme 1: _____

_____

Theme 2: _____

_____

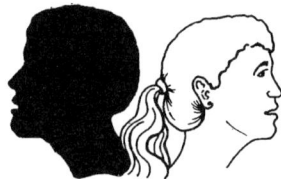

Concerns at School

Part A

Identify two topics that relate to issues or concerns at your school.

Topic 1: _____

Topic 2: _____

Part B

Write a theme that goes with each topic from part A.

Theme 1: _____

_____

Theme 2: _____

_____

Social Justice Concerns

Part A

Identify two topics that relate to social justice concerns facing your community or nation.

Topic 1: _____

Topic 2: _____

Part B

Write a theme that goes with each topic from part A.

Theme 1: _____

_____

Theme 2: _____

_____

Handout 9–B: Permission to reproduce this handout for classroom use is granted.

Music Evaluation

Use the following questions to help you evaluate the music of a prayer service or ritual:

1. How was music used in the opening? ending? reflection time? other parts of the service or ritual?

2. What types of music were used—traditional hymns? modern religious songs? popular music? instrumental music? other? What types of instruments were used—organ? piano? guitar? voice? other? Did these seem to fit in with the rest of the service?

3. In one word, what was your emotional response to the types of music and instruments used? Were you pleased? soothed? stimulated? annoyed? bored? other? Explain.

4. Did the people attending the service participate in the music? If so, how? If not, why not?

5. What was the theme of the service? Did the music create the right mood for the theme?

6. Did the music enhance or take away from your experience of the service? Explain.

7. On a scale from 1 (poor) to 10 (excellent), how do you rate the music of the service overall?

CHAPTER 10

The Eucharist:
Celebrating Jesus' Saving Presence

Section A: Celebrating the Greatest Gift

The first major section of chapter 10 in the student text, pages 153–160, discusses the centrality of the Eucharist to Catholic faith. Through this communal form of prayer, members of the faith community celebrate the gift of Jesus Christ and unite with him in the paschal mystery. The eucharistic liturgy is not a performance to be watched, but an occasion that calls for active participation through listening, singing, and responding with words and actions.

What Do We Bring to God's Table?

Handout 10–A

This individual and group assignment invites students to examine the attitudes they bring to Mass and to reimagine what they can contribute to this celebration.

Give each student a copy of handout 10–A, "At the Lord's Table." Allow the students 10 to 15 minutes to complete the handout. Form small groups of five or six students each and ask the group members to share their handout responses with one another.

A Reflection of What We Bring

This reflection and discussion helps students discover that what we put into the liturgy will greatly affect what we get out of it.

1. Offer this reflection to your students:
- Imagine that you just got free tickets to a concert by a band you have always wanted to see. However, to go to this concert, you must follow these rules:
  —You may not talk louder than a whisper, you may not shout, and, most of all, you may not sing along with the band.
  —You must remain in your seat; no standing or dancing will be permitted.

10

—You may not disturb the band by clapping or waving your hands.

—If you come with someone, you may not sit with that person.

—You may not eat or drink anything during the concert, or buy souvenirs, or wear anything with the band's logo on it.

—You must wear your school clothes. Anyone attending without school clothes will be asked to leave.

Would you want to go to this concert? I did not think so. Many of the things I just said you could not do at this concert are precisely what makes concerts fun—singing and dancing along, being with friends, and dressing up the way you want to for the show.

2. Proceed with a large-group discussion based on this question:
- What comparisons can we make between going to a concert and being able to enjoy it, and attending Mass and feeling good about the experience?

Look for the discussion to bring out the point that the liturgy—whether celebrated as the Mass or another sacrament or as the Divine Office—is not a play or opera that we watch but do not directly participate in. What we get out of the liturgy is a reflection of what we bring to it. If we bring the right attitude and make an effort to participate, the liturgy can be a more meaningful experience for us and for everybody else there.

A Community Ministry

This written reflection exercise stresses the importance of the communal nature of the eucharistic celebration.

Ask your students to describe in their reflection notebook an activity they have participated in that was more meaningful because it was done with other people. Offer an example, such as decorating a Christmas tree with family and friends.

Your students should continue their reflection by responding to these questions and directives:
- Why was this activity more fun to do with a group of people?
- What did you do or say that made the activity a good experience?
- Write about a time when you attended Mass and when you felt that everyone there was really participating—listening, singing, reciting, and sharing together.
- Give three reasons why Mass is more meaningful when shared with others.

Liturgical Ministry

This witness activity encourages students to consider volunteering to help with liturgical ministries at school and in their parish.

If students in your class have served as eucharistic ministers or lectors, or in some other liturgical task, ask several to talk about their experiences with the rest of the class. Advise each of them to prepare a 5-minute talk, using the following questions as a guide:
- Why did you get involved in the first place?
- Why do you continue to serve?

- What were some of the personal fears you had to deal with in order to become more involved in your community's liturgical celebrations?
- How has contributing your gifts affected the way you experience or understand the Eucharist?
- What advice would you give to anyone thinking about volunteering for some sort of liturgical service at their school or parish?

Allow time for questions and discussion after each presentation.

Variation: If no students from your class have served as liturgical ministers at school or in their parish, invite other young adults from the school or local parishes who have done so, to address your class. Offer them the same questions to prepare their talk.

Ten Ways to Get More Out of Mass

Handout 10–B

This reading and reflection urges students to do what they can to get more out of Mass.

Distribute handout 10–B, "Ten Ways to Get More Out of Mass," to your students and assign it for work in class or at home. Instruct your students to read and reflect on the suggestions offered on the handout. Ask them to then think of at least three things they can do to get more out of Mass, and to record these ideas in their reflection notebook. Urge the students to make a firm commitment to follow through with their ideas, to make them personal goals.

After a few weeks, remind the students to revisit their goals and see how they are doing in reaching them.

A Class Mass

A number of the upcoming activities for chapter 10 given in this teaching manual suggest that the students taking this prayer course celebrate a Mass together. Consider concluding the class's work on the Eucharist with a Mass that incorporates as many of these separate activities as feasible.

Invite a priest from your school or neighboring parish to preside at the liturgy. Also, actively involve the students in planning and preparing for this liturgy, encouraging them to combine what they learned about the Eucharist with what they learned about planning communal rituals in chapter 9 of their text.

Section B: The Liturgy of the Word

This section of the student text, pages 160–164, explains that the liturgy of the word was patterned after the Sabbath Scripture service of the ancient Jews. The section takes a close-up look at each part of the liturgy of the word.

The following exercises are designed to increase students' understanding of the different parts of the liturgy of the word:

A Sabbath Service

For a class trip, attend a morning Sabbath service at a local synagogue. Follow up the trip with an in-class discussion focused on these two questions:
- How does the order of the scriptural readings of the Sabbath service compare with the liturgy of the word of the Mass?
- How does the addition of the Gospels and letters to the early Christian communities make this part of the Mass different from the Sabbath service?

Variation: Make this activity an individual out-of-class assignment and require your students to hand in a brief report based on the discussion questions.

Hospitality

Ask your students to jot down three ideas on how to help new students feel welcome at your school. Invite the students to share their ideas during a large-group discussion. Record the ideas on the board, and later create a handout listing the class's ideas and distribute it to the class. Encourage the students to refer to the list the next time a new person joins your school, and to act on one of the ideas. Discuss with the students how a spirit of welcome, or hospitality, has similar effects at school and at Mass.

Greeting

Encourage your students to volunteer to be a greeter at their parish's weekend Mass, welcoming parishioners as they enter the worship space.

Penitential Rite

Write the following example of a "Lord, have mercy" prayer on the board or on an overhead transparency:
- For the times we have treated others poorly and have not given them the respect they deserve.
  Lord, have mercy.
  For the times we thought more about ourselves than about reaching out to others in need.
  Christ, have mercy.
  For the times we got so wrapped up in material things that we forgot what really brings lasting happiness.
  Lord, have mercy.

Split the class into groups of three to four students, and give the groups 10 to 15 minutes to write their own "Lord, have mercy" prayer asking God's forgiveness for themselves or the school community. Randomly select one of the prayers to use in a class liturgy.

Glory to God

Invite your students to write down on a separate piece of paper three ways they can give glory to God through their daily actions. Gather these prayers in a basket and place them before the altar during the recitation or singing of the Gloria in a class Mass.

Proclaiming the Word

Use one or all of the following activities related to the proclamation segment of the liturgy of the word:
- Let the students examine a Sunday lectionary, and explain to them how the readings are organized by seasons of the year and rotate on three cycles.
- Invite a liturgical coordinator from a local parish to give a miniworkshop on the proper way to proclaim—rather than simply read—the word of God.
- Invite the students to form small groups and to proclaim to those in their group the readings for the upcoming Sunday. Encourage the group members to then talk with one another about the connection between the readings and their everyday life.

Second Reading

The second reading of the liturgy of the word usually comes from a letter written to a specific Christian community. Work with your class to write a letter to the next community of students who will take this prayer course. The letter should address this question:
- How are we to live and pray as Christians?

Save the letter and read it to your next prayer course class while working on chapter 10 of the student text.

Gospel and Homily

Do one or both of the following activities:

- Write this prayer on the board or on an overhead transparency, and tell your students to copy the prayer in their reflection notebook:
  - May the word of God fill my mind.

    [Make the sign of the cross on your forehead]

    May my lips always proclaim the word of God.

    [Make the sign of the cross on your lips]

    May the word of God dwell in my heart now and forever.

    [Make the sign of the cross over your heart]

  Invite the students to reflect on the meaning and significance of praying this prayer before hearing the Gospel at Mass. Tell them to record any thoughts that come to mind. Encourage them to pray this prayer during Mass and at any other time they pray with the Scriptures.

- At a class liturgy, ask the presider to engage the students in a dialog homily in which they share their reflections on the Gospel.

Prayer of the Faithful

With the permission of area pastors, ask your students to write a series of petitions to use in the Prayer of the Faithful for next weekend's Mass at their parish. Divide the class into groups by parish, and ask each group to write one series of petitions. Advise the groups to check with their pastor to find out any special events or needs within the parish community that should be included in this series of petitions, and also to decide with the pastor or parish liturgy committee who should read the series of petitions.

Review the completed prayers and, if necessary, offer suggestions for revision. The local pastors may also want to review the prayers ahead of time.

Section C: The Liturgy of the Eucharist

Pages 164–172 of the student text take students through the main parts of the liturgy of the Eucharist to show them that the Eucharist is both a communal meal and a sacrifice.

The following exercises are designed to give students more insight into the different parts of the liturgy of the Eucharist:

Eucharist

If you have access to the *Jesus of Nazareth* video series, watch the segment "Bread of Eternal Life," which is about the Last Supper, with your class. Afterward, allow quiet time for your students to write in their reflection notebook about how they would have felt if they had been one of the Twelve sitting with Jesus and sharing the first Eucharist. For more information on ordering the video, see appendix 2.

Preparation of the Gifts

Do either or both of these activities:
• Ask your students to make or bring a symbol to represent one gift they bring to the table of the Lord. Collect these symbols and place them before the altar during a class liturgy.
• Urge the members of your prayer course to ask everyone in the school to bring a nonperishable food item to the next school liturgy. Direct your class to collect the items, bring them forward during the offertory procession, and deliver them to a local soup kitchen or food pantry that distributes food to poor people.

The Eucharistic Prayer

During a class liturgy, ask the presider to invite your students to join him around the altar for the eucharistic prayer.

The Preface

Study the Gospel passages on Jesus' triumphant entry into Jerusalem, which is the backdrop for the Holy, Holy at Mass: Mark 11:1–11, Luke 19:28–40, and John 12:12–16. Divide the class into three groups and assign each group one of the passages. Let the students refer to a biblical commentary to help them understand these passages. Tell the groups to discuss this question:
• How would you greet Jesus if he visited your town or school today?
Wrap up the discussion by letting the groups share their ideas with the rest of the class.

Calling Down the Spirit

Form seven small groups and assign each group a gift of the Holy Spirit: wisdom, understanding, knowledge, courage, counsel, reverence, and wonder and awe. Give the groups 15 minutes to devise a 2-minute role-play of a situation from their own life where they need the Spirit's help and guidance. Have the groups present their role-play to the rest of the class.

Consecration

Write the following memorial acclamations on the board or on an overhead transparency. Ask your students to pick one, copy it into their reflection notebook, and write a paragraph or two about what the acclamation means to them.
- Christ has died, Christ is risen, Christ will come again.
- Dying, you destroyed our death; rising, you restored our life. Lord Jesus, come in glory.
- When we eat this bread and drink this cup, we proclaim your death, Lord Jesus, until you come in glory.
- Lord, by your cross and Resurrection you have set us free. You are the savior of the world.

Remembrance, Offering, and Intercessions

During a class liturgy, invite each student to light a votive candle in memory of someone who has died. Do this immediately after the Prayer of Remembrance part of the eucharistic prayer is read by the presider. Students should say, "Please remember [the name of the person]," as they light the candle. Everyone else should respond, "We remember."

Great Amen

Review with the class the section "Great Amen" in the student text, pages 168–169. Then read to the class the poem on handout 6–F, "Saying Yes to God and Others," in this manual, page 78. Lead a large-group discussion on ways we can say a great "Amen!" to God every day.

The Lord's Prayer and Sign of Peace

Ask someone to teach your class how to say the Lord's Prayer in sign language and to show your students how to give a sign of peace to one another.

Baking of the Bread

Obtain an approved recipe for making altar bread, from the office of liturgy in your diocese. With your class, bake the bread to be shared later at a class liturgy. Begin your bread making with this prayer:

- We remember and give thanks for all the wonderful people who flavor our life, who knead and mold our values and faith, who encourage us to rise to our potential, and who break bread with us by sharing their life with us.

Communion

Do one or both of the following activities:

- Invite your students to reflect on the prayer "Lord, I am not worthy to receive you, / but only say the word and I shall be healed," and to record their thoughts in their reflection notebook. Encourage them to consider what part of their life needs healing and to bring that need to God in prayer.
- If your students rarely have a chance to receive Communion under the forms of both bread and wine, offer the opportunity at a class liturgy.

Concluding Rite

At the end of a class liturgy, conduct a large-group discussion. Invite your students to consider what concrete things they can do to go forth to love and serve the Lord and one another, especially in light of the Gospel reading from the liturgy.

A Thanksgiving Dinner

Handout 10–C

This written assignment asks students to compare two meals of thanksgiving: the Eucharist and the national holiday dinner celebrated on the last Thursday of November in the United States.

Ask your students to write a two-page essay comparing a traditional Thanksgiving dinner with the Eucharist. Pass out handout 10–C, "A Thanksgiving Dinner," which contains a series of questions to help students focus their essay.

Variation: For extra credit, allow your students to do a longer, more researched report comparing these two meals of thanksgiving.

An Emmaus Walk

This activity asks students to imagine they are the ones who encountered Jesus on the road to Emmaus.

Prepare for the activity by telling your students to bring their Bible to class.

Handout 10–D

Distribute handout 10–D, "The Road to Emmaus: Questions to Walk With," to the class and randomly assign each student a working partner. Instruct the pairs to go outside and to take their Bible and handout with them. Tell them to find a quiet spot to read together the scriptural passage given on the handout, and to then go for a walk and discuss the passage, using the questions on the handout as a springboard. Remind the students to walk only with their assigned partner and to return to your classroom 5 minutes before the class period ends.

Variation: If it is not feasible to allow your students to do this activity outside, let them spread out in the school chapel or gym.

10

At the Lord's Table

Study the characters in this illustration and circle the one that best represents the attitude you bring to Mass. Then answer the following directives and questions and be prepared to discuss your responses:

1. Describe your attitude in words.

2. Why do you feel this way about attending Mass?

3. What do you get out of Mass?

4. Does the attitude you bring to Mass help or hinder what you get out of it? Explain.

5. In what ways could you improve the attitude you bring to Mass so that you receive more from the experience?

Handout 10–A: Permission to reproduce this handout for classroom use is granted.

Ten Ways to Get More Out of Mass

1. Go early; stay late.

Have you ever gone to a movie and missed the first part? That happened to me recently when I went to see "Beauty and the Beast." The line to buy tickets was long . . . and I had to have some popcorn. So I missed finding out how the prince became a beast in the first place. Pretty critical to the story, I'd say.

Jesus has invited you to a banquet. You wouldn't want to offend your host and show up late. You miss a lot in the first few minutes.

Leave enough time to get to church. Find a seat up front, and take time to settle down and pray before Mass starts.

Put your watch away. Stay for the entire Mass. Don't leave after Communion. Sing the closing song. You wouldn't want to leave a party without saying goodbye.

2. Attend with your family or friends.

Mass is a community celebration. Go with your core community, your family. After all this time, there is still truth in the adage "The family that prays together stays together."

I miss going to Mass with my family now that my parents have moved to Florida. They visited for Easter this year, and how grand it was to be together for Easter Sunday liturgy. It was by far the best part of their visit.

Jesus didn't celebrate the Last Supper alone or with one other person. He invited his closest friends to the table. Invite a friend to come with you. Maybe you know of someone whose parents don't attend Mass or who doesn't have a ride. Maybe they just feel funny sitting alone. Invite them to come with you.

3. Get some sleep the night before.

It is hard to concentrate on anything when you are really tired. Remember how Jesus felt when all the Apostles fell asleep in the garden while he was trying to pray.

It must be quite discouraging, too, when the celebrant at Mass looks into the congregation and sees people nodding off. Get to bed a little earlier or go to a later Mass, but make sure you are awake so you don't miss a thing.

4. Participate, participate, participate.

Would you go to a hockey game, sit in the seat farthest from the rink and be very quiet and still through the entire game?

Mass is not a spectator sport. Get off the bench and into the game. Join in the responses and prayers. Kneel, sit and stand at the right times. Sing with the choir even if it isn't your favorite song. Don't worry about your singing ability. God isn't a music critic.

And sit up front, not in the back pew. Even Jesus didn't hang out in Nazareth all his life. He went out to the people, got involved in the community and wasn't afraid to tell people about his father.

5. Listen to the readings.

What do you do when someone has a great story to tell? You move closer, pull up a chair and try to catch every word.

Jesus is a great storyteller. People used to come from all over just to hear him speak. He told stories that touched the lives of his listeners right where they were. The same is still true today.

The Gospel message is written for *you!* Listen to all the readings as if they were written directly to you. Ask yourself "How does this fit into my life?" and "What is Jesus calling *me* to do?"

Reprinted from Maryann Hakowski, in "We Are the Branches," *A.D. Times,* (Diocese of Allentown) (21 May 1992): page 34.

Handout 10–B: Permission to reproduce this handout for classroom use is granted.

133

6. Tune in to the homily.

Priests have a tough time planning homilies when they have an audience of all different ages. It isn't easy coming up with ideas that inspire and excite every week.

Think about the last time you had to write a speech for class and all the time, effort and anxiety you put into getting your point across *and* making it interesting.

Give the homilist a break. Try not to be so critical. Try to see the Scripture passage through his eyes. And if you don't understand the message, take some time after Mass to ask. Most priests are glad to know you were listening and are eager to answer your questions.

7. Receive Communion.

Would you think of going to a friend's house for dinner and refusing to eat anything?

Whenever possible, receive Communion at Mass. And if there is a reason you stay away, get the courage to go to confession. Receiving the Sacrament of Reconciliation is a little less scary when we realize our loving God is waiting with forgiving arms to bring us back to our seat at the banquet table.

Jesus' body and blood are our sources of strength for the journey ahead. His body fills a hunger inside us that no physical bread can ever fill. There is no better way to be closer to Jesus.

8. Pray . . . do it a lot!

Do you make enough time to talk to God? Mass is a great place to pray—as a community and on your own. The responses and special prayers offer opportunities for all kinds of prayer.

During the penitential rite, we pray "Lord, have mercy." Ask God to forgive any hurt you may have caused another in the past week. During the Gloria, we pray "Glory to God in the highest." Take time to praise God for all the wonderful things [God] has done.

During the prayer of the faithful, we pray for special needs in the community. What do you need God's help with right now? The quiet after Communion is a great time to thank God for [God's] many blessings. Count your blessings . . . and remember to say thank you.

9. Get involved.

You have a very important role in the community celebration of liturgy. You need to do more than just "take up space" in the pew for an hour every Sunday. Volunteer to be a lector or join the parish choir. You can even offer to help clean or decorate the church for special feast days.

Whatever promises you make, though, follow through and stick with them. Don't let anyone say you are too young to make a commitment to your church.

10. Come again often.

Make Sunday Mass part of your normal routine. Don't let any other obligation—sports teams, play practice, trips, etc.—interfere with the time you set aside for God.

Take advantage of other opportunities to go to Mass—daily Mass, high school liturgies and special youth group or retreat Masses.

Jesus said: "Do this in remembrance of me." Will you accept his invitation?

A Thanksgiving Dinner

Consider the following questions as you write an essay comparing the Eucharist and the traditional Thanksgiving dinner, celebrated on the last Thursday of November in the United States:

- What do the traditional, secular Thanksgiving dinner and the Eucharist have in common? How are they different?

- What are some of the traditions associated with each meal?

- What makes each meal different from other meals?

- Who is invited to join in each meal?

- What does everyone do before each meal?

- How is the table set? Are special dishes used? What kinds of foods are served?

- Does each meal follow a certain order or pattern? Explain.

- What does everyone do after each meal is over?

- In what other ways can these two meals of thanksgiving be compared?

- How has doing this comparison changed your view of the Thanksgiving dinner? of the Eucharist?

The Road to Emmaus: Questions to Walk With

Read the entire Emmaus story from Luke 24:13–53, and respond to the following questions:

1. Imagine you were one of the disciples who encountered Jesus on the road to Emmaus. What did Jesus say to you?

2. Do you find it hard sometimes to recognize Jesus in the words you hear at Mass? Explain.

3. What are some ways you can recognize Jesus in the other people you break bread with at Sunday Mass?

4. How can you make your encounter with Jesus at Mass as uplifting and joyous as the disciples' encounter with him on the road to Emmaus?

CHAPTER 11

Traditional Prayer: Praying Together in One Voice

Section A: Why Traditional Prayers?

The opening section of chapter 11 of the student text, pages 173–175, advocates a place for traditional prayers in the prayer life of Christians. Traditional prayers reflect the rich history of the Christian community, and in praying them we join our voices with the church of the past, present, and future. Traditional prayers can also be a source of comfort and strength when our own words fail us.

Give Me a *C* . . . Give Me an *H* . . . Give Me an *R* . . .

This activity allows students to see the importance of celebrating in one voice, both when they gather in familiar groups such as for sports and school, and when they celebrate together as a Christian community.

1. Brainstorm with the class a list of anthems, poems, cheers, mottoes, pledges, or songs used by a school or community group. For each example, discuss the following questions:
   • When does the group use or share this example?
   • How does this example contribute to the group's identity?
   • What beliefs does this example express?
   Then pick from the list one or two items that everyone knows the words for, and say or sing them as a class.

2. Brainstorm with the class a list of common prayers and statements of faith used by the Christian community. For each example, discuss the same questions as for step 1 of this activity.
   Then pick from the list one or two items that everyone knows the words for, and say or sing them as a class.

3. Wrap up the activity by discussing the difference between how it feels to do a cheer, say a motto, pray a prayer, and so forth, silently and alone, and how it feels to do this with a group of people.

Look for responses such as these:

- Doing a cheer or professing a creed with others makes it seem more meaningful and more powerful.
- Praying a prayer with others or saying a pledge together creates a strong bond of unity and support among the people.
- When I join with others to pray a prayer like the Lord's Prayer or sing the national anthem, I feel that I belong, that I'm a part of something bigger than myself.
- It's good to have things that everyone knows the words to because then even visitors can join in and feel a part of the celebration or game.

When Words Fail Us

This written reflection activity reinforces the main points of the section "When Words Fail Us" in the student text, pages 174–175.

Give your students their assignment by saying the following:

- At times we just cannot find the words to say or write what we are feeling. Sometimes we buy flowers or a greeting card or a gift to express what we want to say. Often the deepest feelings, such as sorrow when a loved one dies or unconditional love for someone, are the hardest to convey.

  Like the flowers or the greeting cards or the gifts, many prayers of the church seem to say what we need to say at just the right moment. For example, we may say the Act of Contrition when we are deeply sorry, pray the Prayer of Praise when we are grateful for a special blessing, or repeatedly recite the Hail Mary when we are lonely, scared, and in need of a friend.

  In your reflection notebook this evening, describe a special greeting card you sent or received that said just the right thing at the right moment. Include what the card looked like, what it said (as best you can remember), and what it meant to you.

  Next, write the words of at least one traditional prayer and describe how it helped you pray in the past or how it may help in the future.

Section B:
The Lord's Prayer: From the Heart of Jesus

Pages 175–182 of the student text unfold the rich meaning of the Lord's Prayer as the summary of Jesus' teachings about relating to God and others. The prayer begins by acknowledging the bond between ourselves and God. The next three phrases draw us to God's glory; the remaining four help us bring our needs before God.

A Prayer for All God's People

This research project helps students discover the universality of the Lord's Prayer.

Working in groups of three, your students are to research and learn how to say and write the Lord's Prayer in another language. Give the groups a week to do their research. Tell them to prepare to recite the prayer in their selected foreign language to the class and to submit to you a written version. Challenge the class to use as many languages as possible. If a student already knows more than one language, urge that student to choose an unfamiliar language.

When the students have completed their research, spend a class period letting the groups share the Lord's Prayer in the many languages they have discovered. Close by emphasizing the universality of the Lord's Prayer—how its message crosses the borders of countries and the barriers of language differences.

Variation: Compile the written foreign-language versions of the Lord's Prayer into a booklet for students, or post them on a classroom bulletin board.

Many Prayers in One Prayer

This written exercise invites students to explore the different types of prayer found in the Lord's Prayer and to respond to parts of the prayer that relate to their life.

Handout 11–A

Give each student a copy of handout 11–A, "Many Prayers in One Prayer," and instruct the class to complete the handout individually. When everyone has completed their handout, ask them to share their answers in groups of four.

God, Our Mother and Our Father

This discussion challenges students to think beyond the image of God as Father and to reflect on the image of God as Mother.

After your students have read the section "Our Father Who Art in Heaven" in the student text, page 176, invite them to pray the Lord's Prayer substituting "Our Mother" for "Our Father" at the start of the prayer.

Observe their reactions and lead a large-group discussion with the following questions:

- How did you feel about praying "Our Mother" instead of "Our Father" at the beginning of the Lord's Prayer? Why?
- How does addressing God as our Mother change how you understand and relate with God?
- A number of passages from the Hebrew Scriptures use the image of a mother to represent God. Jesus would have been familiar with these passages. Why, then, did Jesus address God as Father instead of Mother in the prayer he taught his followers?
- Why is it important that we not limit our images of God?
- What other images of God could we substitute for father or mother in the Lord's Prayer?

Variation 1: Ask your students to write the Lord's Prayer starting with "Our Mother" in their reflection notebook and to record their reactions.

Variation 2: Allow your students to substitute other biblical images for God, such as king, judge, shepherd, creator, or warrior, and talk about how their feelings about the prayer change.

Destination: Heaven

This small-group activity asks students to reflect on their view of heaven and stresses that heaven is not a place, but a way of being.

1. Bring to class about a dozen large pieces of construction paper or lightweight poster board or card stock, sets of multicolored markers, pairs of scissors, and dispensers of glue. Ask each student to bring a few travel brochures and magazines to class.

2. Divide the class into groups of five to six students each. Give one piece of the large paper to each group and ask the group to fold it in thirds, like a simple travel brochure. Distribute the markers, scissors, and glue among the groups.

3. Pass along these instructions to the groups:
- For today, you are no longer students. Instead, you work for the promotions department of a travel agency. You have just received a tough assignment: to create a travel brochure for heaven. Your slogan for the brochure can be one of the following phrases:
—Heaven is a way of being.
—Love, and give the world a glimpse of heaven.
   To make your brochure, you may cut out words and pictures from the brochures and magazines you brought to class, as well as use your own artwork. Have fun and be creative.

4. Give the groups about 20 minutes to create their brochure. Ask a spokesperson from each small group to share the group's creation with the entire class. Display the heaven brochures in the classroom for the remaining time that your students work with chapter 11.

Praise Graffiti

This activity invites students to reflect on the many ways we take God's name in vain and offers them an opportunity to give praise to God.

1. Before the students arrive for class, cover one wall of your classroom with butcher paper. Write, "Holy Is Your Name," in very large letters across the top of the paper. Have several packs of colored markers available.

2. Begin the activity with a large-group discussion on the following questions:
- How do we take God's name in vain through our words?
- How do we take God's name in vain through our actions?
- What are some words or phrases that take God's name in vain and that are so commonly used that we may not even realize they do so?
- How can our inaction or omissions hurt the name of God?
- How can listening to certain songs or watching certain movies diminish the holiness of God's name?

3. Proceed by saying the following to the class:
- Graffiti are a common form of expression used by those who are angry, want to make a public statement, and have no other release for their

emotions. Besides destroying public or private property, this negative expression often lashes out at God and people.

But writing in public places need not always be a negative and destructive form of expressing one's feelings. Today, we are going to do something called praise graffiti. This is a chance for you to share your feelings of gratitude and thanksgiving toward God in a public statement.

Pause for a moment to think of a slogan or phrase that honors God's name or gives praise to God. Then write your message anywhere on the paper on the wall. You may write large or small, choose any color marker, and even decorate your message if you wish. You do not have to sign your name, but you can if you want. This praise graffiti wall is our prayer for today.

The Kingdom Is Now

This scriptural study of parables found in the Gospels helps students learn more about the Reign of God we pray for in the Lord's Prayer.

Ask your students to bring their Bible to class. Divide the class into five groups and assign each group one of the following scriptural passages:
- Matthew 13:44
- Matthew 13:45–46
- Matthew 13:47–50
- Mark 4:30–32
- Luke 13:20–21

The groups are to read their scriptural passage and be prepared to share with the rest of the class the answers to the following questions:
- To what does Jesus compare the Reign of God in your parable?
- What is he trying to tell us about the Reign through your parable?
- Based on the lesson of your parable, what can we do to help build the Reign of God?

You may want to write these questions on the board for easy reference.

Your Will Be Done, God

Handout 11–B

This written reflection invites students to make prayer an important part of their decision-making process.

Distribute handout 11–B, "Your Will Be Done, God," and ask your students to follow the instructions given on the handout. This reflection activity may be done during class or at home.

Encourage your students to seek God's will in all their decisions. Advise them to keep this handout in their reflection notebook for future reference.

Many Breads, One Community

This prayer service reminds students that God, through many people, gives us daily bread to satisfy our physical and spiritual hunger. It invites us in North America to join with the wider community of the world in bringing our needs before God and celebrating one another's gifts.

Preparation

1. Purchase one package each of rice cakes, flour tortillas, and pita bread, and an unsliced loaf each of rye bread and wheat bread.

On the day of the service, line a large basket with a clean dish towel, and fill it with the loaves of rye bread and wheat bread and with several pieces of each other type of bread. Place the basket in the center of a worship space where your students can sit on the floor in a circle.

Handout 11–C

2. Ask six readers to prepare the bread blessings and scriptural reading on handout 11–C, "Many Breads, One Community." You or a student can take the role of leader.

Provide each of readers 1 to 5 with a small, flat wicker basket or a dinner plate. Give them these instructions to follow during the service: They are to take from the center basket the bread that corresponds with their reading (for example, reader 1 will take the rice cakes), put it in their small basket or on their plate, and hold the bread while they read the blessing. After they read the blessing, they should break off a small piece of bread to eat, and then pass the small basket or plate around the circle so that each person can share in the bread.

Procedure

Begin by explaining to the class that they will be praying the Lord's Prayer in a special way that symbolizes their unity in Christ with all the peoples of the world. Proceed with the prayer service described on handout 11–C. (Only the leader and the six student readers need a copy of handout 11–C.)

As We Forgive Others

This activity invites students to connect Jesus' teachings about forgiveness to their own life.

Ask your students to bring their Bible to class for this activity. Pair up the students and tell them to do the following:
1. Reread the parable of forgiveness, about Tess and her sister, found on page 181 in the student text, and discuss its message.
2. Read and discuss Matt. 18:21–35.
3. Share with one another a story about forgiveness—or the lack of it—from their own life.

Triumph over Evil

This out-of-class assignment asks students to see beyond the bad news of evil-doers to discover the good news created by persons living and working in their community.

Instruct your students to scan the local newspapers or other media to find a story about someone who makes a positive difference in their community. Ask the students to write a short essay about how God works through this person to "deliver us from evil."

Variation 1: Ask your students to interview a person who brings good into their community and to write up a summary of that interview.

Variation 2: Brainstorm with your students on ways they can deliver the world from evil.

Section C: Prayers of Faith in the Trinity

Pages 182–185 in the student text stress the importance of the Trinity in Christian prayer. The Sign of the Cross is one of the first prayers we are taught as children, and we pray the Apostles' Creed as a summary of our beliefs about God. The Spirit, all too often overlooked in prayer, can be addressed as our Advocate and Counselor.

Praying in God's Name

This discussion challenges students to think about what they mean when they pray:

In the name of the Father,
and of the Son,
and the Holy Spirit. Amen.

Begin by asking your students to pray the Sign of the Cross. They will likely do it very quickly. Ask them to do it again slowly and more reverently, thinking about each word as they say it. Then, conduct a discussion based on the following questions:

- Who taught you how to make the sign of the cross?
- How many times do you think you have made the sign of the cross in your life?
- What are some occasions when you made the sign of the cross or saw others doing it?
- Do you ever feel awkward or embarrassed about making the sign of the cross in public, especially when you are not in church? Why or why not?
- What does it mean to preface a prayer by making the sign of the cross?
- What does it mean to say we are doing something in the name of the Father, the Son, and the Holy Spirit?
- What are some things you would like to start doing in God's name?

Do You Live What You Believe?

This mock trial requires students to examine how they do or do not live out the beliefs they profess when they pray the Apostles' Creed.

1. Prepare for this activity by asking a student who is good at mediating to serve as the judge of a mock trial. Also, write each of the three parts of the Apostles' Creed on a separate piece of paper and place the three parts in a bag. (See page 184 of the student text for the words of the Apostles' Creed.)

2. On the day of the trial, divide the class into three groups and allow each group to choose a piece of paper from the bag. Give the groups 10 minutes to prepare their defense for how their school or local community lives out this part of the Apostles' Creed.

3. Instruct the person playing the role of judge to ask one group these questions:

- What do you believe? *[Tell the group to read the part of the creed assigned to it]*
- How do you live what you believe? *[Ask the group to give examples that demonstrate how its school or community lives out its stated beliefs]*

Direct the rest of the class to play devil's advocate for the group, formally presenting to the court negative examples from the school or community that go against this belief. Instruct the judge to then ask the group to refute the charges, or, if they are true, to offer ways for the school or community to correct this inconsistency.

4. Repeat step 3 for the remaining two groups.

Called by the Spirit

Handout 11–D

This small-group activity asks students to identify ways Christians are answering the call of the Spirit to "renew the face of the earth."

Give each student a copy of handout 11–D, "Called by the Spirit," and review the instructions with the class.

Allow the students several days to a week to find their examples, and then ask them to share some of their findings in class.

Section D: Prayers to and with Mary

This section of the student text, pages 185–190, discusses the special place Mary, the mother of Jesus, has in the heart and prayers of Catholic Christians. Mary is the person many Catholics turn to in times of crisis or when they are in need of healing. The Hail Mary, Magnificat, and rosary are among the prayers of praise and intercession used to ask Mary to draw us closer to her Son and our Lord, Jesus.

A Mother and Much More

This research project helps students examine the many images of Mary and why Catholic Christians throughout the ages have found her so approachable that they can come to her with their deepest concerns and prayers.

Let your students work in pairs to collect information about prayers to Mary used by Christians throughout the history of the church, or about images or legends associated with her. From their research, the pairs should choose one particular prayer, image, or legend and, in a report, summarize the history of its use and its meaning. They should also discuss in that report their personal response to their selection.

Powerful Devotion

This witness talk allows students to experience vicariously a pilgrimage to a shrine in devotion to Mary, and how God's grace works through her to cure those broken in body and spirit.

Invite someone who has made a pilgrimage to Lourdes, France, the shrine to Our Lady of Guadalupe in Mexico City, or some other pilgrimage site to speak to your class. Ask them to talk about the history of the place, the special meaning it has to pilgrims, the deep faith they found in the people they met there, and the effect of the pilgrimage on their spiritual life—how Mary has helped them grow closer to Jesus and to God.

Allow plenty of time for your students to ask questions of the speaker.

Meditating on the Mysteries

This written reflection activity invites students to pray the rosary on their own and take time to reflect on the mysteries of the Gospel associated with the rosary.

Ask your students to choose the joyful, sorrowful, or glorious mysteries, listed on page 189 of their text. Each night for five nights, they are to pray a decade of the rosary, read the scriptural passage for one of the mysteries under their chosen category, and write in their reflection notebook their thoughts on the meaning of the mystery.

At the end of the five nights, encourage the students to continue praying the rosary on their own and reflecting on the other two sets of mysteries.

Variation: If some students are unfamiliar with praying the rosary, you may want to review pages 187–190 in the student text and pray the rosary together as a class. If any students do not have their own rosary beads, find some for them to borrow.

Many Prayers in One Prayer

The Lord's Prayer includes three forms of prayer: praise, petition, and promise. Identify the type or types of prayer for each phrase of the Lord's Prayer, and then respond to the directives that follow the prayer.

Type of Phrase

Our Father who art in heaven, _____

hallowed be thy name. _____

Thy kingdom come. _____

Thy will be done on earth, as it is in heaven. _____

Give us this day our daily bread, _____

and forgive us our trespasses, _____

   as we forgive those who trespass against us, _____

and lead us not into temptation, _____

but deliver us from evil. _____

For the kingdom, the power
   and the glory are yours, now and forever. _____

Amen. _____

1. Write a personal response to one of the petitions you found in the Lord's Prayer.

2. Write a personal response to one of the praises you found in the Lord's Prayer.

3. Write a personal response to one of the promises you found in the Lord's Prayer.

Your Will Be Done, God

Use the following guide to help you discover God's will for you on a decision you face. Write your responses in your reflection notebook.

1. Think of a decision you must make right now.
    Tell God about this decision.

2. How do you feel about this decision?
    Share these feelings with God.

3. What are some of the pros and cons of your decision?
    Explain these pros and cons to God.

4. How will your decision affect other people?
    Discuss the needs of these people with God.

5. What examples from the life or teachings of Jesus relate to your decision?
    Share your insights with God.

6. What do you think is God's will for you in this decision?
    Let God speak to you through your feelings and thoughts.

7. What decision have you made?
    Ask God to help you follow through on your decision.

Many Breads, One Community

Leader: Please join hands and pray the Lord's Prayer together, stopping after the phrase "Give us this day our daily bread." *[The leader starts praying the Lord's Prayer]*

Reader 1: God of everlasting life, bless these rice cakes, fruit of the harvest of countries in Asia. May the taste of rice remind us of the hard work of those who toil in the fields and work for excellence in other areas. Keep us ever mindful of the Asian people who richly gift our culture with their traditions and heritage. Unite us in prayer with them in the blessing and eating of these rice cakes. *[All share in the eating of the rice cakes]*

Reader 2: Creator of the harvest, bless these tortillas, fruit of Latin America. May the taste of tortilla remind us of those who live close to our own homeland and the many who struggle to rise above poverty. Keep us ever mindful of the people of Latin America who richly gift our culture with their traditions and heritage. Unite us in prayer with them in the blessing and eating of these tortillas. *[All share in the eating of the tortillas]*

Reader 3: God of freedom and justice, bless this pita bread, a gift to us from Africa and the Middle East. May the taste of pita remind us of the struggles for freedom in many of these lands, and of the land from which Jesus came. Keep us ever mindful of the people of Africa and the Middle East who richly gift our culture with their traditions and heritage. Unite us in prayer with them in the blessing and eating of this pita bread. *[All share in the eating of the pita bread]*

Reader 4: Grantor of Wisdom, bless this rye bread, a gift from the countries of Europe. May the rich taste of this bread be a reminder of those who settled our country many years ago. Keep us ever mindful of the people of Europe who richly gift our culture with their traditions and heritage. Unite us in prayer with them in the blessing and eating of this rye bread. *[All share in the eating of the rye bread]*

Reader 5: Sustainer God, from whom comes the abundance of the harvest, bless this wheat bread, fruit of the toil of the American farmer. May the taste of this bread remind us of the struggles of the farmer, of those who are paid too little to bake and package the bread, and of those in our country who cannot afford to buy even bread to eat. Keep us ever mindful of all the people in our midst who richly gift our daily life. Unite us in prayer with them in the blessing and eating of this wheat bread. *[All share in the eating of the wheat bread]*

Reader 6: Then Jesus said to them, "Very truly, I tell you, it was not Moses who gave you the bread from heaven, but it is my Father who gives you the true bread from heaven. For the bread of God is that which comes down from heaven and gives life to the world." They said to him, "Sir, give us this bread always."

Jesus said to them, "I am the bread of life. Whoever comes to me will never be hungry, and whoever believes in me will never be thirsty. But I said to you that you have seen me and yet do not believe. Everything that the Father gives me will come to me, and anyone who comes to me I will never drive away; for I have come down from heaven, not to do my own will, but the will of him who sent me. And this is the will of him who sent me, that I should lose nothing of all that he has given me, but raise it up on the last day. This is indeed the will of my Father, that all who see the Son and believe in him may have eternal life; and I will raise them up on the last day." (John 6:32–40)

Leader: Let's join hands again and continue praying the Lord's Prayer. *[The leader continues, "and forgive us our trespasses . . ."]*

Handout 11–C: Permission to reproduce this handout for classroom use is granted.

Called by the Spirit

The Spirit is active and working to help us "renew the face of the earth." We are challenged to go forth to make peace, serve one another, act justly, heal the sick, and relieve suffering.

Search the periodicals and other resources in the library or media center at school or in your local public library for examples from around the world of Christians doing the work of the Spirit. Find an example for each of the five categories listed here, and prepare a summary of each example to share in class.

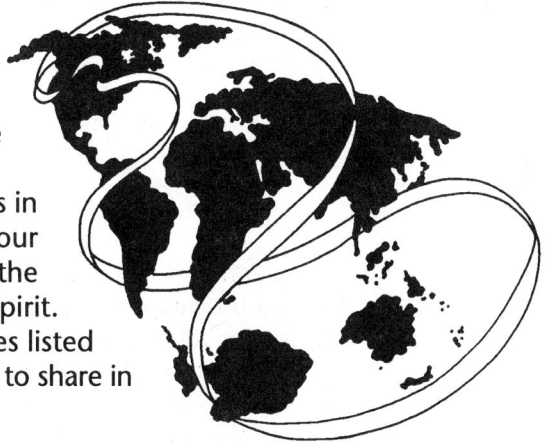

Make Peace

Serve One Another

Act Justly

Heal the Sick

Relieve Suffering

Growing in a Life of Prayer

In the epilogue of the student text, pages 191–196, students are urged to reflect on their experience of prayer during the course and to identify the prayer styles they are most comfortable with. Prayer is a process through which, with time and patient practice, we open our heart to allow God to work within us. Through prayer, we grow in faith, finding peace as we learn to place our trust in God. We grow in hope, finding good in a world overrun with evil. And we grow in love, allowing God's love to transform us and be manifest through us.

Prayer Is . . .

This revisitation of the exercise "Prayer Is . . . " in this teaching manual, page 13, asks students to examine how their attitudes about prayer have changed through the course.

On one of the last days of the course, ask your students to take out a piece of paper and a pen or pencil. Tell them you will write a sentence starter on the board and they will have 5 minutes to jot down their responses.

• On the board, write, Prayer is . . .

After 5 minutes, invite the students to share their responses, and record these on the board.

After everyone has had a chance to share their thoughts, read they responses they gave for this activity at the beginning of the course. Ask the students to identify how their attitudes about prayer have changed.

Prayer Changes People

This written reflection activity invites students to examine how this course has expanded their view of prayer and how prayer has affected them since the beginning of this course.

1. Ask your students to respond to the following questions in their reflection notebook:
   • How has your prayer changed?
   • How has prayer changed you?

Give the students about 15 minutes' writing time and then invite them to share some of their responses with the rest of the class.

2. After the sharing time, stress to your students the value of continuing to write in a journal after this course ends. You may want to say something like this:

- Your reflection notebook has been a constant companion throughout this prayer course. My hope is that you have found the journal-writing activities helpful and enjoyable and that you will continue to write in your journal, even when this class is over.

  During this course, the subjects and methods for journal writing were set for you. Now it is your turn to decide what to write about and how. Look for opportunities for reflection in your everyday experiences and encounters with the Sacred. Feel free to review chapter 6 of your text occasionally to refresh your memory on the different ways to use a journal. When you fill up your current reflection notebook, start writing in another one. Journal writing, or reflective writing, is a great way to keep your prayer life vital and growing.

Closing Prayers

This written exercise invites students to draw upon the different styles of prayer they experienced during the course, to compose their own closing prayer.

As a home assignment, instruct your students to choose one of the styles of prayer they experienced during the course and to compose their own closing prayer for the course. Encourage them to focus their prayer around one of the following themes found in the epilogue of their text:

- Prayer changes people.
- Pray from the heart.
- Grow in faith, hope, and love.
- My life is in God's hands.
- Slow me down, Lord.

Tell the students to write their prayer in their reflection notebook.

Closing Liturgy

An appropriate way to end this prayer course would be to celebrate a eucharistic liturgy prepared by the students. The liturgy could weave together some of the separate elements from the course into a single prayer experience. Here are some suggestions for doing this, to share with your students:

Music: Review with your students the "Different Ways to Praise" activity in this manual, page 59. Suggest that they use the list for ideas on including a variety of musical styles and traditions in the liturgy.

Penitential rite: Let your students choose from among the "Lord, have mercy" prayers they wrote while working with chapter 10 (see page 126 in this manual).

Responsorial psalm: Use handout 2–A, "Creation Praise: Psalm 148" in this manual, page 28. Or allow your students to choose some other psalm that better suits their chosen theme for the liturgy and the other readings.

Second reading: Use the letter answering the question How are we to live and pray as Christians? that your students were asked to write to next year's prayer course participants as part of their work with chapter 10 (see page 126 of this manual).

Homily: Suggest that your students share snippets of their favorite homilies, which they may have written about for the "Homily Collection" activity in this manual, page 69.

Prayer of the Faithful: Refer your students to the "Shared Prayer" activity in this manual, page 118, for ideas for the shared prayer portion of this liturgy.

Preparation of the gifts: Bring forth the thank-you notes your students wrote for the "Praising and Thanking God" activity in this manual, page 113. If your students have not done that activity, urge them to write a thank-you note in preparation for this liturgy.

Remembrance segment of the eucharistic prayer: Use handout 4–C, "Litany of the Saints," in this manual, page 55. Or ask your students to write their own litany calling on deceased loved ones to pray for them.

Communion: Make your own eucharistic bread as suggested in the activity "Baking of the Bread" in this manual, page 130.

Variation: Instead of ending the course with a eucharistic liturgy, hold a prayer service in which each student shares her or his personal closing prayer (from the preceding activity, "Closing Prayers," in this manual) with the rest of the class. Consider composing your own closing prayer and sharing it at this time as well.

Course Evaluation

Handout 12–A

To help you more effectively teach this course in the future, give your students an opportunity to evaluate their experience of it. Use handout 12–A, "Course Evaluation," or put together an evaluation of your own. Ask your students to complete their course evaluation and hand it in before they leave on the last day of class.

Course Evaluation

Please answer the following questions honestly and legibly. Your comments are appreciated and will help to improve this course.

1. Are you glad you took this course? Please explain.

2. List some of the activities you found most worthwhile and tell why you liked them.

3. Which activities seemed lacking? Please explain.

4. Did you find the large class discussions helpful? the small-group discussions? Why or why not?

5. Did you find the written reflection exercises valuable? Please explain.

6. Of all the prayer experiences you participated in during this course, which one did you find the most meaningful? Why?

7. Which chapter of the student text was most helpful? Why?

8. Which chapter of the student text was least helpful? Why?

9. If you could teach this class to next year's students, how would you change it?

Appendices

APPENDIX 1

Resources for Teaching *PrayerWays*

Boelhower, Gary J. *Sacred Times, Sacred Seasons*. Milwaukee, WI: Hi-Time Publishing, 1986.

Brokamp, Marilyn. *Prayer Times for Intermediate Grades*. Cincinnati, OH: St. Anthony Messenger Press, 1987.

Caprio, Betsy. *Experiments in Prayer*. Notre Dame, IN: Ave Maria Press, 1973.

Cavanaugh, Brian. *The Sower's Seeds*. New York: Paulist Press, 1990.

_____. *More Sower's Seeds*. New York: Paulist Press, 1992.

Glory and Praise, classic edition. Phoenix, AZ: North American Liturgy Resources, 1990.

Hakowski, Maryann. *Pathways to Praying with Teens*. Winona, MN: Saint Mary's Press, 1993.

_____. *Vine and Branches*. Volumes 1, 2, and 3. Winona, MN: Saint Mary's Press, 1991–94.

Jessie, Karen. *Seasonal Liturgies: Senior High–Young Adult*. Villa Maria, PA: Center for Learning, 1987.

Jessie, Karen, Kimberly A. Langley, and Robert W. Meaney. *Prayer Service Models*. Villa Maria, PA: Center for Learning, 1989.

Koch, Carl, ed. *Dreams Alive: Prayers by Teenagers*. Winona, MN: Saint Mary's Press, 1991.

_____. *More Dreams Alive: Prayers by Teenagers*. Winona, MN: Saint Mary's Press, 1995.

Link, Mark. *The Psalms for Today*. Allen, TX: Tabor Publishing, 1989.

_____. *You: Prayer for Beginners and Those Who Have Forgotten How*. Niles, IL: Argus Communications, 1976.

McKee, William F. *Listen with Your Heart: Five-Minute Meditations*. Liguori, MO: Liguori Publications, 1987.

Moore, Joseph. *Monday Morning Jesus: Turning Your Retreat into Everyday Living*. Ramsey, NJ: Paulist Press, 1984.

Neary, Donal. *The Calm Beneath the Storm: Reflections and Prayers for Young People*. Chicago, IL: Loyola University Press, 1983.

O'Malley, William J. *Daily Prayers for Busy People*. Winona, MN: Saint Mary's Press, 1990.

Reeves, Sr. John Maria, and Sr. Maureen Roe. *Junior High Liturgy, Prayer, Reconciliation*. Villa Maria, PA: Center for Learning, 1988.

Reutemann, Charles. *Let's Pray!* Winona, MN: Saint Mary's College Press, 1975.

_____. *Let's Pray/2*. Winona, MN: Saint Mary's Press, 1982.

Simsic, Wayne. *Earthsongs: Praying with Nature*. Winona, MN: Saint Mary's Press, 1992.

Songs of Praise, combined edition. Ann Arbor, MI: Servant Music, 1982.

APPENDIX 2

Sources for Recommended Audiovisuals

Chapter 1
The film *One Who Was There* is available for rental ($30) from Mass Media Ministries, 2116 North Charles Street, Baltimore, MD 21218; 800-828-8825 or 301-727-3270.

Chapter 2
The CD or tape *Say Yes* can be ordered from Heartbeat Records; call 800-433-3262.

Chapter 7
Order the video *Jingo* from Franciscan Communications/St. Anthony Messenger Press, 1615 Republic Street, Cincinnati, OH 45210-1298.

Chapter 10
Jesus of Nazareth, directed by Franco Zeffirelli, is sold in fourteen segments, which are available separately ($29.95 each) or as a complete set ($289.95). For more information, contact Don Bosco Multimedia, 475 North Avenue, P.O. Box T, New Rochelle, NY 10802-0845; 800-342-5850 or 914-576-1024.

Acknowledgments *(continued)*

The scriptural quotations contained herein are from the New Revised Standard Version of the Bible. Copyright © 1989 by the Division of Christian Education of the National Council of the Churches of Christ in the United States of America. All rights reserved.

The words from *The Cloud of Unknowing* on page 12 are as quoted in "Back to Basics: Moral Reasoning and Foreign Policy 'after Containment,'" by George Weigel, in *Peacemaking: Moral and Policy Challenges for a New World*, edited by Gerard F. Powers, Drew Christiansen, and Robert T. Hennemeyer (Washington, DC: United States Catholic Conference [USCC], 1994), page 69. Copyright © 1994 by the USCC, Washington, DC. All rights reserved.

The stories "Where Are You, Lord?" by Brewer Mattocks, on handout 2–D and "Believe It, Achieve It," by Mark Link, on handout 6–D are from *More Sower's Seeds: Second Planting,* by Brian Cavanaugh (New York: Paulist Press, 1992), pages 8–9 and 76, respectively. Copyright © 1992 by Brian Cavanaugh. All rights reserved. Used by permission of Paulist Press.

The English translation of the Litany of the Saints on handout 4–C and the "Lord, I am not worthy" prayer on page 130 are from *The Roman Missal,* translated by the International Commission on English in the Liturgy (ICEL) (New York: Catholic Book Publishing Company, 1985), pages 196–197 and 564, respectively. Copyright © 1973 by the ICEL. All rights reserved. Used by permission.

"The Serenity Prayer," by Reinhold Niebuhr, on handout 6–C is as quoted in *Familiar Quotations,* fifteenth edition, by John Bartlett (Boston: Little, Brown and Company, 1980), page 823. Copyright © 1882, 1891 by John Bartlett. Copyright © 1910, 1914, 1919, 1942 by Anna Sprague DeWolf and Louisa Bartlett Donaldson. Copyright © 1937, 1948, 1955, 1965, 1968, 1980 by Little, Brown and Company. All rights reserved.

The illustration on handout 6–G is inspired by Joseph Moore, *Monday Morning Jesus: Turning Your Retreat into Everyday Living* (New York: Paulist Press, 1984), page 51. Copyright © 1984 by Joseph Moore. All rights reserved.

The prayer on handout 6–H is from William J. O'Malley, *Daily Prayers for Busy People* (Winona, MN: Saint Mary's Press, 1990), page 86. Copyright © 1990 by Saint Mary's Press, 702 Terrace Heights, Winona, MN 55987-1320. All rights reserved.

The psalm "A Lamentation," by Jennifer Filkins, on page 101 is from *Dreams Alive: Prayers by Teenagers,* edited by Carl Koch (Winona, MN: Saint Mary's Press, 1991), page 12. Copyright © 1991 by Saint Mary's Press, 702 Terrace Heights, Winona, MN 55987-1320. All rights reserved.

Handout Masters

List of Handout Masters

Handouts

Open the Book on Your Own Story

Answer the following questions in marker on the outside of your blank book cover. Make your cover look like a real book jacket: put your title, the answer to question 1, on the front; put the answers for questions 2 to 8, in complete sentences, on the back or on the inside flaps.

1. If you were to write a book about your life, what would be the title?

2. Where does your story begin?

3. Who are the most important characters in your book?

4. What are some of the settings for your story?

5. What is one high point in your story?

6. What is one low point in your story?

7. Where does God fit into your story?

8. What do you expect to happen to you next?

Through the Eyes of Faith

Complete the following sentences in the spaces provided:

1. If I put on the eyes of faith, **my family** would look . . .

2. If I put on the eyes of faith, **tough decisions** would look . . .

3. If I put on the eyes of faith, **my friends** would look . . .

4. If I put on the eyes of faith, **my schoolwork** would look . . .

5. If I put on the eyes of faith, **my problems** would look . . .

6. If I put on the eyes of faith, **my prayer life** would look . . .

7. If I put on the eyes of faith, **my future** would look . . .

Behind the Picket Fence

1. On the pickets of the fence, write down the qualities you let others see about yourself, or the qualities you would like others to see.

2. On the spaces between the pickets, write down the qualities about yourself that you tend to hide from others.

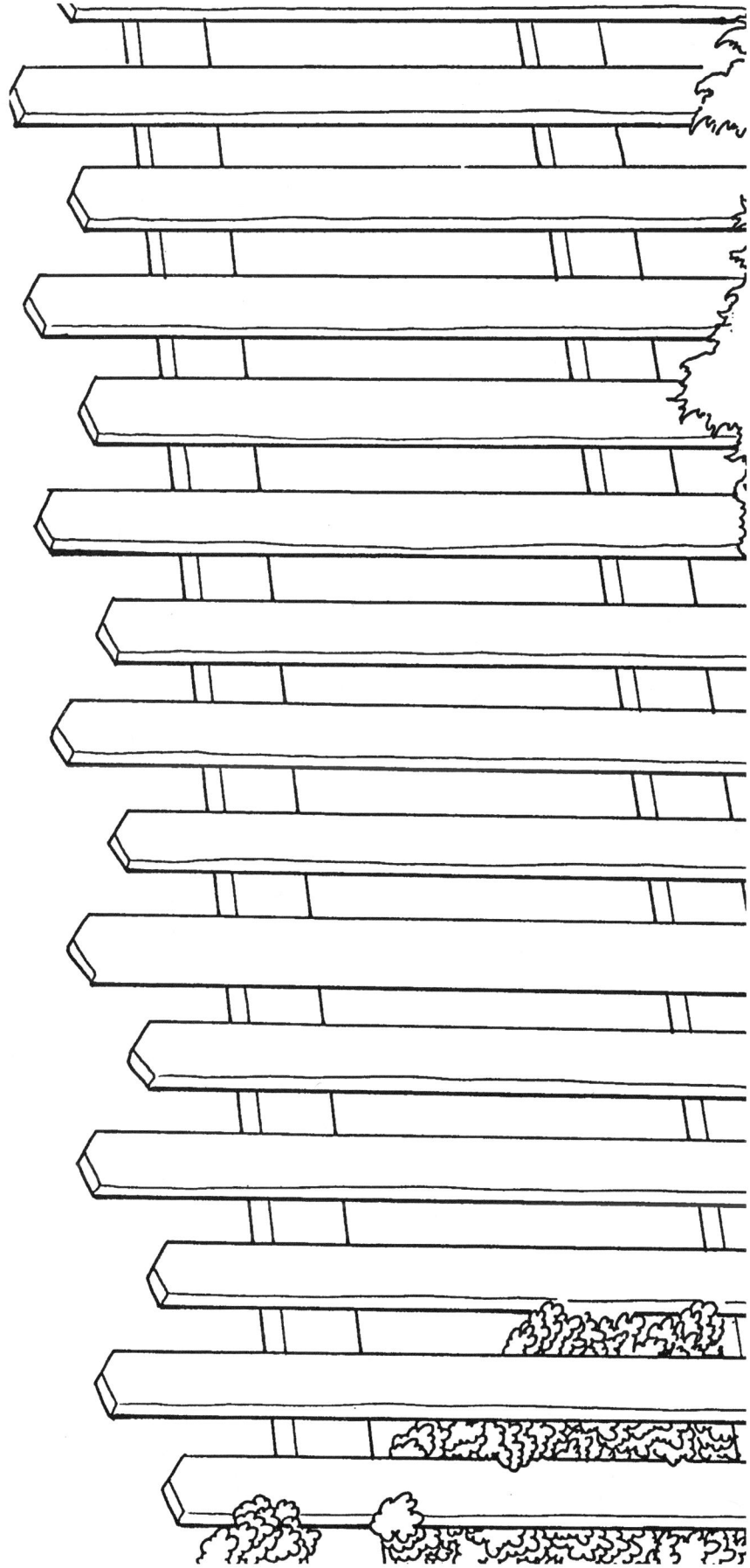

A Sample Kaleidoscope Image

Use this image as a model to make the kaleidoscope poster for the kaleidoscope prayer service.

Voices for
"A Kaleidoscope Prayer Service"

Hidden Colors

Voice 1: I can't talk to my parents anymore; no one has time to listen to me.

Voice 2: I am doing worse and worse in chemistry class. I just know I am going to flunk my next test.

Voice 3: I want to ask Sharon to the dance, but I am afraid she will turn me down.

Voice 4: I really want to play on the basketball team. What will I do if I don't make the first cut?

Voice 5: My parents are always bugging me to go to church on Sunday, but what if my friends see me there?

Voice 6: I don't want to go to that party—I know people will be drinking there. But I don't want to sit home alone.

True Colors

Voice 1: Mom, can we talk? It's really important. Can you make some time for me?

Voice 2: Ms. Brown, I'm really struggling with chemistry, but I'd like to do better. Would you help me find a tutor?

Voice 3: Sharon, would you like to go to the dance with me? We could stop for some pizza afterward.

Voice 4: I think I'll play some basketball at the Y; I'll practice every day so I'll be ready for the tryouts.

Voice 5: John, why don't we go together to the youth group Mass this Sunday. Maybe we will meet some new people there.

Voice 6: Sue, are you worried about what might happen at this party, too? Why don't we go see a movie instead?

Finding God in Others

Attentively read this story. Then take a few moments to reflect quietly on its meaning. On the back of this handout, write about some ways you can find the Lord in your classmates and family, and in the world around you.

Where Are You, Lord?

The parish priest in a town named Austerity climbed way up in the church's steeple to be nearer to God. He wanted to hand down God's Word to his parishioners, like Moses of old. Then, one day he indeed thought he heard God say something.

The priest cried aloud from the steeple, "Where are you, Lord? I can't seem to hear your voice clearly."

And the Lord replied, "I'm down here among my people. Where are you?"

(Brewer Mattocks, from Brian Cavanaugh,
More Sower's Seeds, pages 8–9)

Creation Praise: Psalm 148

All: Praise the LORD!

Right: Praise the LORD from the heavens;
praise him in the heights!

Left: Praise him, all his angels;
praise him, all his host!

Right: Praise him, sun and moon;
praise him, all you shining stars!

Left: Praise him, you highest heavens,
and you waters above the heavens!

Right: Let them praise the name of the LORD,
for he commanded and they were created.

Left: He established them forever and ever;
he fixed their bounds, which cannot be passed.

Right: Praise the LORD from the earth,
you sea monsters and all deeps,

Left: fire and hail, snow and frost,
stormy wind fulfilling his command!

Right: Mountains and all hills,
fruit trees and all cedars!

Left: Wild animals and all cattle,
creeping things and flying birds!

Right: Kings of the earth and all peoples,
princes and all rulers of the earth!

Left: Young men and women alike,
old and young together!

Right: Let them praise the name of the LORD,
for his name alone is exalted;
his glory is above earth and heaven.

Left: He has raised up a horn for his people,
praise for all his faithful,
for the people of Israel who are close to him.

All: Praise the LORD!

(Psalm 148)

On the back of this handout, jot down ways the psalm
illustrates how God is present in creation.

Who Is Your God?

Here are some statements people use to describe God. Some may be familiar, others not. Place a check mark before the ones you agree with; place an *X* before the ones you disagree with.

___ the only person who loves me for myself
___ the computer that programs the universe
___ a puppeteer who manipulates people like toys
___ an energy people discover when a baby is born or they fall in love
___ an unseen universal soul people are a part of
___ a creator who believes that everything created is good
___ a force that was active during biblical times but not today
___ a father who loves his children selflessly
___ a mother who nurtures her children
___ someone who forgives all my mistakes
___ a being beyond my words or understanding
___ an eccentric being who created the world and forgot about it
___ someone who dares to let me be free
___ a being who gave me life
___ a lawgiver who commands me to do right, not wrong
___ a ruler whose power is freedom and love, rather than force
___ a lover who invites me to a heavenly marriage feast
___ an idea created by past generations to explain the world
___ the peace bringer who will reign when people are as sisters and brothers
___ the perfect one who makes me feel guilty
___ the one who wants me to become myself
___ a cosmic clown who created joy and laughter
___ other (specify) _____
___ other (specify) _____

Images of Jesus in the Scriptures

Read the following passages and identify the image of Jesus used in each:

1. John 1:29   _____
2. Luke 22:27   _____
3. Revelation 19:16   _____
4. Isaiah 9:6   _____
5. Acts 2:36   _____
6. 1 Peter 5:4   _____
7. John 11:25   _____
8. Luke 4:24   _____
9. Mark 4:1–2   _____
10. Hebrews 2:11   _____
11. John 6:51   _____
12. 1 Timothy 1:1   _____
13. Matthew 8:2–3   _____

Praise Cards

Spend some time reflecting about the many ways God, Jesus, and the Holy Spirit have blessed you. Then, using the forms provided here, compose prayers of praise and thanksgiving for these many blessings.

O Jesus,

I praise and thank you
for

_____

_____

_____

_____

_____

_____

_____

O Spirit,

I praise and thank you
for

_____

_____

_____

_____

_____

O God,

I praise and thank you
for

_____

_____

_____

_____

_____

_____

"Knock . . ."

Knocker: *[Knock, knock, knock]*
Reader: Come in, with your dreams.

Knocker: *[Knock, knock, knock]*
Reader: Enter, carrying your wishes and your longings.

Knocker: *[Knock, knock, knock]*
Reader: Open the door, you who are afraid or worried, or weighed down.

Knocker: *[Knock, knock, knock]*
Reader: Bring your dreams, bring your hopes, bring your burdens.

Knocker: *[Knock, knock, knock]*
Reader: Bring them all here to be blessed and made holy.

Knocker: *[Knock, knock, knock]*
Reader: Bring them to me because they are *you.*

Knocker: *[Knock, knock, knock]*
Reader: Welcome. Be at home. Come in.

Prayer Is a Two-Way Street

Write your responses to the following questions and directives in your reflection notebook:

1. Describe a time when you prayed for something but did not seem to get a response.

2. Describe a time when God answered your prayer but in a way you did not expect.

3. Write a prayer for a need you have right now.

4. How can you take action with God to meet this need?

5. How might God respond to your prayer?

Litany of the Saints

Leader	Respondents
Lord, have mercy	Lord, have mercy
Christ, have mercy	Christ, have mercy
Lord, have mercy	Lord, have mercy
Holy Mary, Mother of God	pray for us
Saint Michael	pray for us
Holy angels of God	pray for us
Saint John the Baptist	pray for us
Saint Joseph	pray for us
Saint Peter and Saint Paul	pray for us
Saint Andrew	pray for us
Saint John	pray for us
Saint Mary Magdalene	pray for us
Saint Stephen	pray for us
Saint Ignatius	pray for us
Saint Lawrence	pray for us
Saint Perpetua and Saint Felicity	pray for us
Saint Agnes	pray for us
Saint Gregory	pray for us
Saint Augustine	pray for us
Saint Athanasius	pray for us
Saint Basil	pray for us
Saint Martin	pray for us
Saint Benedict	pray for us
Saint Francis and Saint Dominic	pray for us
Saint Francis Xavier	pray for us
Saint John Vianney	pray for us
Saint Catherine	pray for us
Saint Teresa	pray for us
All holy men and women	pray for us
Lord, be merciful	Lord, save your people
From all evil	Lord, save your people
From every sin	Lord, save your people
From everlasting death	Lord, save your people
By your coming as man	Lord, save your people
By your death and rising to new life	Lord, save your people
By your gift of the Holy Spirit	Lord, save your people
Be merciful to us sinners	Lord, hear our prayer

The Eucharist as Praise

Examine all the parts of the Eucharist in the missalette. Using the spaces provided on this handout, identify and discuss three prayers or parts of the liturgy that praise and thank God.

Example 1

Prayer or part of the liturgy:

Excerpts of the prayer or of the part of the liturgy:

How does this prayer or part of the liturgy help us praise and thank God?

Example 2

Prayer or part of the liturgy:

Excerpts of the prayer or of the part of the liturgy:

How does this prayer or part of the liturgy help us praise and thank God?

Example 3

Prayer or part of the liturgy:

Excerpts of the prayer or of the part of the liturgy:

How does this prayer or part of the liturgy help us praise and thank God?

Looking Back on the Road of Life

"Give thanks in all circumstances." (1 Thessalonians 5:18)

Complete the following statements in the spaces provided:

4. Other people helped me
get through it by . . .

_____

_____

_____

_____

2. When this happened,
I felt . . .

_____

_____

_____

_____

5. This time may have been
a blessing in disguise
because . . .

_____

_____

_____

_____

3. God helped me get
through this time by . . .

_____

_____

_____

_____

1. A time when suffering
touched my life was . . .

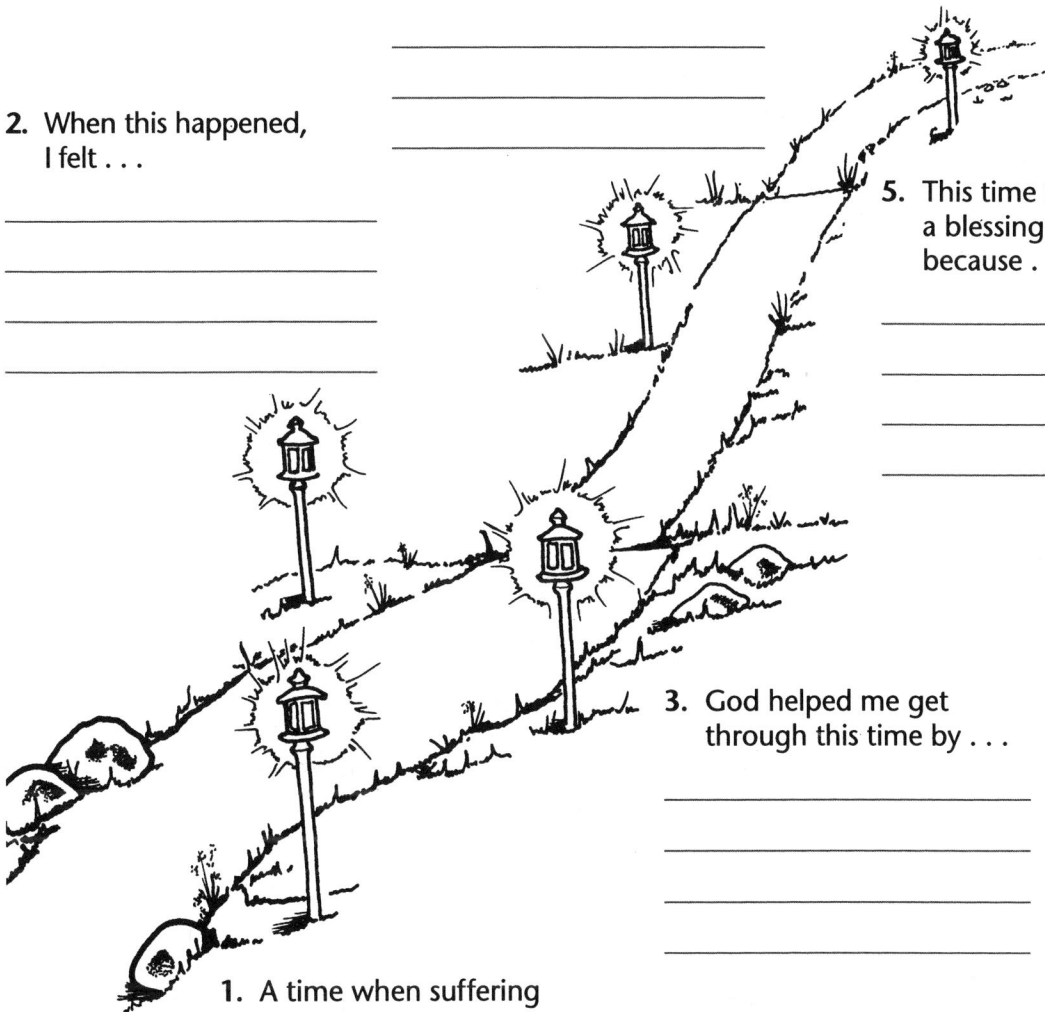

_____

_____

_____

Tell Me About a Joyful Experience

Base your interview on the following questions. Record the interview directly on this handout or in your reflection notebook.

1. Please describe a situation in which you experienced joy.

2. Is there a special reason that this experience was joyful for you? If so, what?

3. Did this joyful experience change your life in any way? If so, how?

4. Do you feel that God was working in this experience? Please explain.

5. Did you thank God for this experience? If so, how?

A Time for Everything

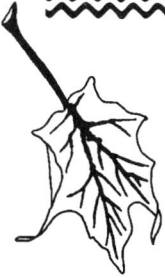

Read this scriptural passage and respond to the reflection questions and directives that follow it:

> For everything there is a season, and a time for every matter under heaven:
>
> a time to be born, and a time to die;
> a time to plant, and a time to pluck up what is planted;
> a time to kill, and a time to heal;
> a time to break down, and a time to build up;
> a time to weep, and a time to laugh;
> a time to mourn, and a time to dance;
> a time to throw away stones, and a time to gather stones together;
> a time to embrace, and a time to refrain from embracing;
> a time to seek, and a time to lose;
> a time to keep, and a time to throw away;
> a time to tear, and a time to sew;
> a time to keep silence, and a time to speak;
> a time to love, and a time to hate;
> a time for war, and a time for peace.
>
> (Ecclesiastes 3:1–8)

For Reflection

- List some things for which now is the appropriate time in your life. Explain why you feel this way.

- Describe the hardest time in your life so far. Why was it so hard?

- Describe the best time in your life so far. Why was it so good?

Taking Off the Masks

Complete these statements and then respond to the reflection questions that follow them:

The masks I wear when I am with others are . . .

The real me is . . .

For Reflection

• Why is it sometimes hard to take off our masks and allow our true self to come through?

• Are there situations when it seems appropriate to put on a mask? If you think so, name several such situations and discuss why a mask is appropriate for them. If you think masks are never appropriate, explain why.

A Prayer for Serenity

Read this prayer and respond to the reflection questions that follow it:

The Serenity Prayer

God, give us grace to accept with serenity the things that cannot be changed, courage to change the things which should be changed, and the wisdom to distinguish the one from the other.

(Reinhold Niebuhr, in John Bartlett, *Familiar Quotations,* page 823)

For Reflection

- What things in your life right now do you need to change? Ask God for the courage to make those changes.

- What things in your life right now cannot be changed and are tough to accept? Ask God for the strength to accept what cannot be changed.

- How do you know which things to change and which to accept? What criteria do you use? What signs might help you decide? Ask God for the wisdom to make this decision.

You Have to Believe

Read this story and respond to the reflection questions that follow it:

Believe It, Achieve It

In the "Star Wars" movie, *The Empire Strikes Back,* Luke Skywalker flies his X-wing ship to a swamp planet on a personal quest. There he seeks out a Jedi master named Yoda to teach him the ways of becoming a Jedi warrior. Luke wants to free the galaxy from the oppression of the evil tyrant, Darth Vader.

Yoda reluctantly agrees to help Luke and begins by teaching him how to lift rocks with his mental powers.

Then, one day, Yoda tells Luke to lift his ship out from the swamp where it sank after a crash landing. Luke complains that lifting rocks is one thing, but lifting a star-fighter is quite another matter. Yoda insists. Luke manages a valiant effort but fails in his attempt.

Yoda then focuses his mind, and lifts out the ship with ease. Luke, dismayed, exclaims, "I don't believe it!"

"That's why you couldn't lift it," Yoda replied. "You didn't believe you could."

(Mark Link, in Brian Cavanaugh, *More Sower's Seeds,* page 76)

For Reflection

• What are some things you would like to achieve?

• What do you need to believe in, in order to accomplish what you want in life?

• What are some areas in which you lack self-confidence?

• How can faith in God help you build faith in yourself?

• How can faith in God help you achieve your goals?

Answering a Letter

Imagine yourself as a first-century Christian from the Asia Minor city of Colossae. The Christian community in Colossae has just received a letter from the Apostle Paul. The following is a segment of that letter. Read it carefully and then write a letter back to Paul.

> As God's chosen ones, holy and beloved, clothe yourselves with compassion, kindness, humility, meekness, and patience. Bear with one another and, if anyone has a complaint against another, forgive each other; just as the Lord has forgiven you, so you also must forgive. Above all, clothe yourselves with love, which binds everything together in perfect harmony. And let the peace of Christ rule in your hearts, to which indeed you were called in the one body. And be thankful. Let the word of Christ dwell in you richly; teach and admonish one another in all wisdom; and with gratitude in your hearts sing psalms, hymns, and spiritual songs to God. And whatever you do, in word or deed, do everything in the name of the Lord Jesus, giving thanks to God the Father through him. (Colossians 3:12–17)

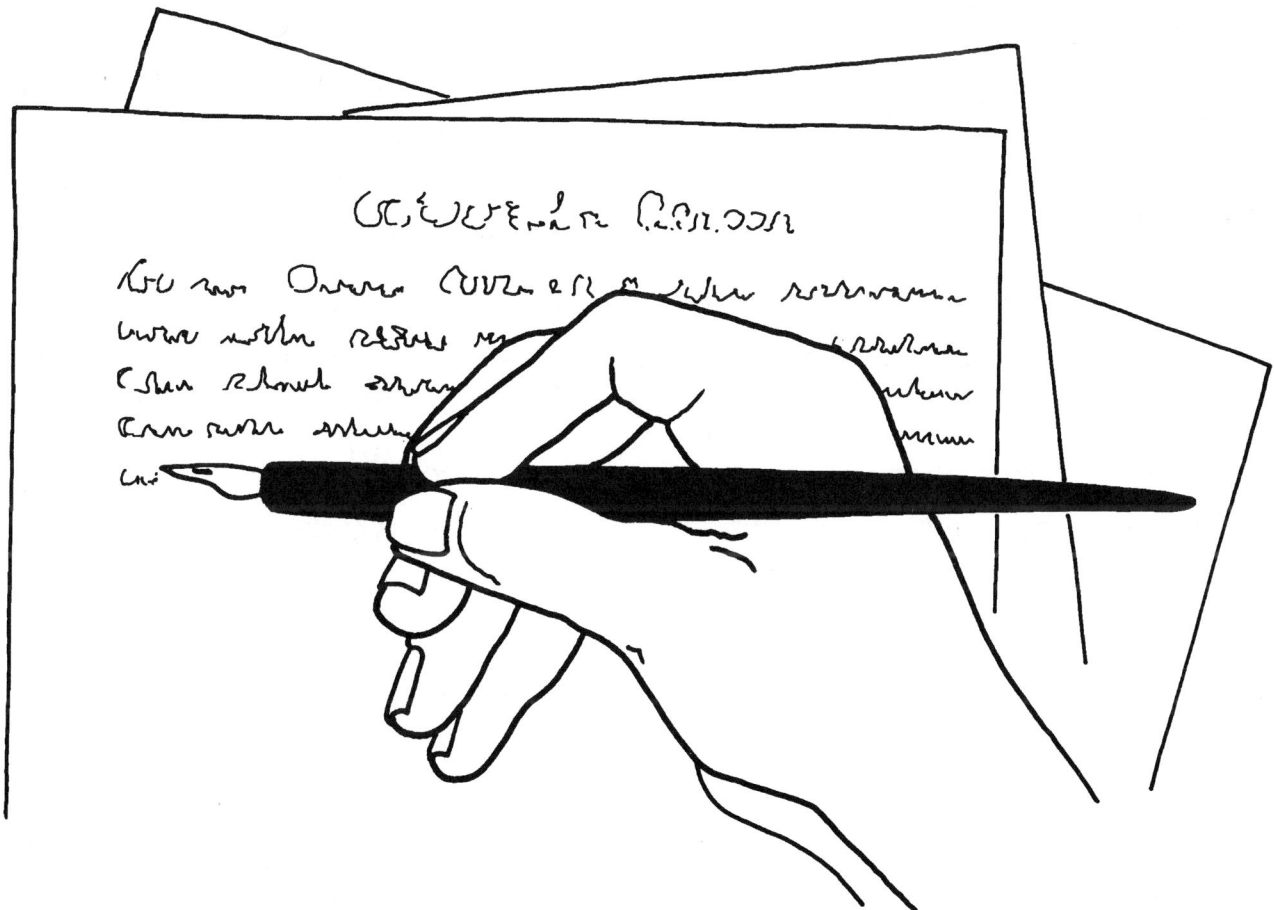

Saying Yes to God and Others

Read this poem, "Saying Yes to God and His People," and respond to the reflection questions that follow it:

Saying yes to God and his people is a good
    thing.

Saying yes to God is adoration.
It's awareness.
It's understanding.
It's prayer
It's reassurance.
It's faith.

Worry
Pain
Loss
Inhumanity
Betrayal
Sin
Lack of concern
Indifference

Horror
    tend to tie the yessing tongue.
Tied tongues can always be untied.

Peace
Grace
Glory
    follow.

People too need yesses.
All the time.
People need to know that they are
    worthwhile.
Yes reassures them.
People are weak.
Yes supplies strength.

Saying yes may be

    a nod
    a smile
    a tear
    a being there

    a hand
    a loving
    a walking with
    a talking to
    a listening
    a saying no.

Where people end and God begins is hard to see.
Ofttimes God and people are the same.

Dapple each day with yesses.
Greet morn and eve with a yes.

Saying yes is godliness.

(William F. McKee, *Listen with Your Heart,* pages 9–10; originally published in *Ligourian,* May 1985. Reprinted with permission from *Ligourian,* One Liguori Drive, Liguori, MO 63057.)

For Reflection

- How can you say yes to God?

_____

_____

_____

_____

_____

_____

_____

- How can you say yes to others?

_____

_____

_____

_____

_____

_____

_____

What Now?

Imagine yourself in the predicament of the person in this illustration. You must decide, What am I going to do now? After studying the situation for a few moments, proceed with the reflection questions and directives following the illustration.

So it's gonna be a prayer group, huh?

For Reflection

- First write your gut response.

- Then write what you think the "logical" response should be.

- Finally, consider your response if you put on the heart and mind of Jesus and responded in the way you think Jesus would.

- How does this third response compare with the first two?

I Am No Longer a Child

Read this prayer, at the same time imagining yourself as its author, and then respond to the reflection questions and directives that follow it:

> Living God,
> I am no longer a child.
> You will not do my work,
> play the game for me,
> fight my battles.
> So be it,
> as long as you cheer me on the way.
> (William J. O'Malley, *Daily Prayers for Busy People,* page 86)

For Reflection

• What does growing up mean to you?

• What fears do you have about growing up?

• Do you welcome any aspects of growing up? If so, what are they?

• Write a prayer asking God's help as you grow into adulthood.

What Can Meditation Do for Me?

Complete the following sentences:

1. The five adjectives that best describe me are . . .

2. My favorite way to pray is . . .

3. One weakness of my prayer life is . . .

4. Given who I am and my approach to prayer, I will benefit from meditation because . . . (list at least five reasons)

5. Meditation will challenge me to . . .

6. One thing that makes me nervous about meditating is . . .

Meditation and Mass

Use the process described on this handout as a way to get more out of the next Mass you attend. Familiarize yourself with the process by reading over the steps several times before you attempt to do them.

   1. Arrive ten minutes before the liturgy starts. Settle into an appropriate and comfortable prayer posture and concentrate on opening yourself up to God.

   2. Close your eyes and imagine yourself seated in a calm, peaceful place inside your heart. Invite God into your heart and ask that you will be open to the message in the liturgy of the word and to the gift of Jesus the Christ in the Eucharist.
   Any time you find yourself being distracted by the people coming and taking their seats around you, gently travel back to your place of calm and peace.

   3. During the liturgy, let your heart and your mind focus on the richness of the symbols in the eucharistic celebration. Let yourself experience that celebration as if for the first time.

   4. When the Mass is over, stay for five minutes after everyone else leaves. Prayerfully reflect on the message of God's word and the experience of receiving Jesus in the Eucharist. Give thanks to God for these gifts.

The Scriptures as Literature

Search through the Hebrew Scriptures and the Christian Testament to find an example of each of the following literary styles. Record the exact location of the example, and summarize its main message.

Style	Citation	Message
Story		
Legend		
Myth		
History		
Conversation		
Letter		
List		
Biography		
Law		
Speech		
Poem		
Parable		
Proverb		
Advice		
Wise teaching		
Song		
Prayer		

Prayerful Symbols

In each passage listed here, the Gospel writer John uses a symbol to teach readers something important about Jesus. For each passage, read the verse or verses in your Bible, write down the symbol used for Jesus, and answer these two questions:
1. What does this symbol teach us about Jesus?
2. How can this symbol help us relate to Jesus?

John 1:29–31

John 6:25–40

John 8:12

John 10:7–16

John 15:1–5

Songs for Every Need

From your assigned list, identify the psalms that reflect each of the following types of themes. Note that some psalms contain only one theme type, whereas others express several.

Praise Psalms (Giving Glory to God)

Wisdom Psalms (Offering a Guide for Human Conduct)

Royal Psalms (Asking God's Guidance for the King)

Thanksgiving Psalms (Expressing Gratitude for Blessings)

Lamentation Psalms (Crying Out in Woe and Misfortune)

Witness Talk on the Parable of the Lost Sheep

Prepare a witness talk centering around the parable of the lost sheep, Luke 15:1–7. Read or creatively retell the parable at some point in your talk, probably the beginning.

Reflect on the following questions and directives as you prepare your witness talk. Feel free to structure and shape your talk as you see fit. In other words, it is not at all necessary for your talk to follow the order of these questions and directives.

- At baptism we were accepted into the Christian community. How does the Good Shepherd continue to call us to be part of the flock? Is it possible to be lost within the flock?
- What are some ways people get lost today? (For example, through drugs, alcohol, video games, overwork.)
- Describe a time when you felt lost.
- Contrast the feelings of acceptance and rejection.
- Identify people who have helped you feel that you belong.
- Why is a sense of belonging important to your self-worth?
- How can you keep others from feeling left out? How can you invite them to be part of our community of Christians?
- How can you help others experience Jesus, the good shepherd?
- Identify the feelings associated with these activities in the parable: losing, seeking, finding, rejoicing.
- How do the symbols in the parable of the lost sheep speak to you?

General Guidelines

Here are some general guidelines for preparing and giving a witness talk:
- Share your feelings; be open and honest.
- Share examples and stories from your own life.
- Speak slowly and thoughtfully.
- Prepare an outline of your talk, but do not read word for word.
- Practice giving the talk to someone, and ask for feedback.
- Try to keep eye contact with your listeners.
- Use a scriptural passage, song, or poem to help make your point.
- Try to keep your talk to fifteen to twenty minutes.
- End with a challenge or something for listeners to think about.
- Most important, be yourself.

Go Out to All the World

Reader 1: Luke 2:1–12
All: Go out to all the world and tell the Good News.

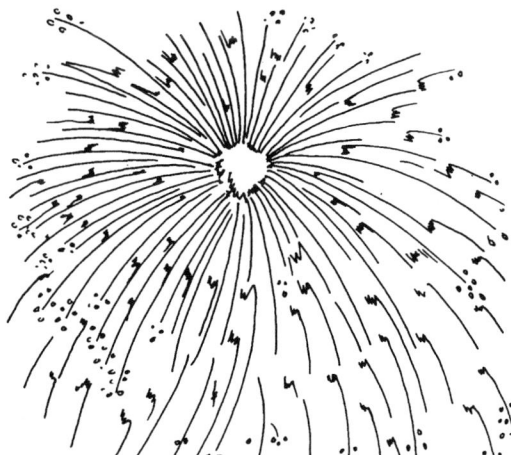

Reader 2: John 4:6–9
All: Go out to all the world and tell the Good News.

Reader 3: John 2:1–5
All: Go out to all the world and tell the Good News.

Reader 4: John 9:6–7
All: Go out to all the world and tell the Good News.

Reader 5: Mark 8:6–9
All: Go out to all the world and tell the Good News.

Reader 6: Luke 4:40–41
All: Go out to all the world and tell the Good News.

Reader 7: Matthew 9:20–22
All: Go out to all the world and tell the Good News.

Reader 8: John 11:39–44
All: Go out to all the world and tell the Good News.

Reader 9: Luke 17:12–14
All: Go out to all the world and tell the Good News.

Reader 10: Mark 14:22–24
All: Go out to all the world and tell the Good News.

Reader 11: Matthew 28:5–10
All: Go out to all the world and tell the Good News.

My Favorite Celebration

Reflect on all the celebrations you have been a part of or witnessed, and choose your favorite. Feel free to think of celebrations in as wide a sense as you want. They may be as elaborate and organized as a wedding, or as simple as a special picnic with your family. They may be a one-time occasion, such as the baptism of a sibling, or an annual occasion, such as a Christmas pageant. They may be as nonpersonal as the opening ceremonies of the Olympics, or as personal as your sixteenth birthday party.

Once you have decided on your favorite celebration, respond to the following directives and questions:

1. Briefly describe your favorite celebration and give some reasons why it is your favorite.

2. Pick one ritual associated with your favorite celebration and answer these questions about some of its main details:

   a. What particular words or sayings are part of the ritual? Why?

   b. What actions are part of the ritual? Why?

   c. What symbols are key to the ritual? What do the symbols stand for?

3. Summarize what your celebration would be like without this ritual.

From Topic to Theme

Seasons of the Year

Part A
Identify two topics that relate to the seasons of the year.

Topic 1: _____

Topic 2: _____

Part B
Write a theme that goes with each topic from part A.

Theme 1: _____

_____

Theme 2: _____

_____

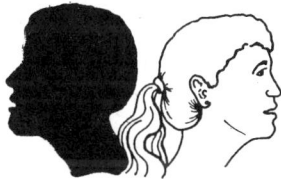

Concerns at School

Part A
Identify two topics that relate to issues or concerns at your school.

Topic 1: _____

Topic 2: _____

Part B
Write a theme that goes with each topic from part A.

Theme 1: _____

_____

Theme 2: _____

_____

Social Justice Concerns

Part A
Identify two topics that relate to social justice concerns facing your community or nation.

Topic 1: _____

Topic 2: _____

Part B
Write a theme that goes with each topic from part A.

Theme 1: _____

_____

Theme 2: _____

_____

Music Evaluation

Use the following questions to help you evaluate the music of a prayer service or ritual:

1. How was music used in the opening? ending? reflection time? other parts of the service or ritual?

2. What types of music were used—traditional hymns? modern religious songs? popular music? instrumental music? other? What types of instruments were used—organ? piano? guitar? voice? other? Did these seem to fit in with the rest of the service?

3. In one word, what was your emotional response to the types of music and instruments used? Were you pleased? soothed? stimulated? annoyed? bored? other? Explain.

4. Did the people attending the service participate in the music? If so, how? If not, why not?

5. What was the theme of the service? Did the music create the right mood for the theme?

6. Did the music enhance or take away from your experience of the service? Explain.

7. On a scale from 1 (poor) to 10 (excellent), how do you rate the music of the service overall?

At the Lord's Table

Study the characters in this illustration and circle the one that best represents the attitude you
bring to Mass. Then answer the following directives and questions and be prepared to discuss
your responses:

1. Describe your attitude in words.

2. Why do you feel this way about attending Mass?

3. What do you get out of Mass?

4. Does the attitude you bring to Mass help or hinder what you get out of
it? Explain.

5. In what ways could you improve the attitude you bring to Mass so that
you receive more from the experience?

Ten Ways
to Get More Out of Mass

1. Go early; stay late.

Have you ever gone to a movie and missed the first part? That happened to me recently when I went to see "Beauty and the Beast." The line to buy tickets was long . . . and I had to have some popcorn. So I missed finding out how the prince became a beast in the first place. Pretty critical to the story, I'd say.

Jesus has invited you to a banquet. You wouldn't want to offend your host and show up late. You miss a lot in the first few minutes.

Leave enough time to get to church. Find a seat up front, and take time to settle down and pray before Mass starts.

Put your watch away. Stay for the entire Mass. Don't leave after Communion. Sing the closing song. You wouldn't want to leave a party without saying goodbye.

2. Attend with your family or friends.

Mass is a community celebration. Go with your core community, your family. After all this time, there is still truth in the adage "The family that prays together stays together."

I miss going to Mass with my family now that my parents have moved to Florida. They visited for Easter this year, and how grand it was to be together for Easter Sunday liturgy. It was by far the best part of their visit.

Jesus didn't celebrate the Last Supper alone or with one other person. He invited his closest friends to the table. Invite a friend to come with you. Maybe you know of someone whose parents don't attend Mass or who doesn't have a ride. Maybe they just feel funny sitting alone. Invite them to come with you.

3. Get some sleep the night before.

It is hard to concentrate on anything when you are really tired. Remember how Jesus felt when all the Apostles fell asleep in the garden while he was trying to pray.

It must be quite discouraging, too, when the celebrant at Mass looks into the congregation and sees people nodding off. Get to bed a little earlier or go to a later Mass, but make sure you are awake so you don't miss a thing.

4. Participate, participate, participate.

Would you go to a hockey game, sit in the seat farthest from the rink and be very quiet and still through the entire game?

Mass is not a spectator sport. Get off the bench and into the game. Join in the responses and prayers. Kneel, sit and stand at the right times. Sing with the choir even if it isn't your favorite song. Don't worry about your singing ability. God isn't a music critic.

And sit up front, not in the back pew. Even Jesus didn't hang out in Nazareth all his life. He went out to the people, got involved in the community and wasn't afraid to tell people about his father.

5. Listen to the readings.

What do you do when someone has a great story to tell? You move closer, pull up a chair and try to catch every word.

Jesus is a great storyteller. People used to come from all over just to hear him speak. He told stories that touched the lives of his listeners right where they were. The same is still true today.

The Gospel message is written for *you!* Listen to all the readings as if they were written directly to you. Ask yourself "How does this fit into my life?" and "What is Jesus calling *me* to do?"

Reprinted from Maryann Hakowski, in "We Are the Branches," *A.D. Times,* (Diocese of Allentown) (21 May 1992): page 34.

6. Tune in to the homily.

Priests have a tough time planning homilies when they have an audience of all different ages. It isn't easy coming up with ideas that inspire and excite every week.

Think about the last time you had to write a speech for class and all the time, effort and anxiety you put into getting your point across *and* making it interesting.

Give the homilist a break. Try not to be so critical. Try to see the Scripture passage through his eyes. And if you don't understand the message, take some time after Mass to ask. Most priests are glad to know you were listening and are eager to answer your questions.

7. Receive Communion.

Would you think of going to a friend's house for dinner and refusing to eat anything?

Whenever possible, receive Communion at Mass. And if there is a reason you stay away, get the courage to go to confession. Receiving the Sacrament of Reconciliation is a little less scary when we realize our loving God is waiting with forgiving arms to bring us back to our seat at the banquet table.

Jesus' body and blood are our sources of strength for the journey ahead. His body fills a hunger inside us that no physical bread can ever fill. There is no better way to be closer to Jesus.

8. Pray . . . do it a lot!

Do you make enough time to talk to God? Mass is a great place to pray—as a community and on your own. The responses and special prayers offer opportunities for all kinds of prayer.

During the penitential rite, we pray "Lord, have mercy." Ask God to forgive any hurt you may have caused another in the past week. During the Gloria, we pray "Glory to God in the highest." Take time to praise God for all the wonderful things [God] has done.

During the prayer of the faithful, we pray for special needs in the community. What do you need God's help with right now? The quiet after Communion is a great time to thank God for [God's] many blessings. Count your blessings . . . and remember to say thank you.

9. Get involved.

You have a very important role in the community celebration of liturgy. You need to do more than just "take up space" in the pew for an hour every Sunday. Volunteer to be a lector or join the parish choir. You can even offer to help clean or decorate the church for special feast days.

Whatever promises you make, though, follow through and stick with them. Don't let anyone say you are too young to make a commitment to your church.

10. Come again often.

Make Sunday Mass part of your normal routine. Don't let any other obligation—sports teams, play practice, trips, etc.—interfere with the time you set aside for God.

Take advantage of other opportunities to go to Mass—daily Mass, high school liturgies and special youth group or retreat Masses.

Jesus said: "Do this in remembrance of me." Will you accept his invitation?

A Thanksgiving Dinner

Consider the following questions as you write an essay comparing the Eucharist and the traditional Thanksgiving dinner, celebrated on the last Thursday of November in the United States:

- What do the traditional, secular Thanksgiving dinner and the Eucharist have in common? How are they different?

- What are some of the traditions associated with each meal?

- What makes each meal different from other meals?

- Who is invited to join in each meal?

- What does everyone do before each meal?

- How is the table set? Are special dishes used? What kinds of foods are served?

- Does each meal follow a certain order or pattern? Explain.

- What does everyone do after each meal is over?

- In what other ways can these two meals of thanksgiving be compared?

- How has doing this comparison changed your view of the Thanksgiving dinner? of the Eucharist?

The Road to Emmaus: Questions to Walk With

Read the entire Emmaus story from Luke 24:13–53, and respond to the following questions:

1. Imagine you were one of the disciples who encountered Jesus on the road to Emmaus. What did Jesus say to you?

2. Do you find it hard sometimes to recognize Jesus in the words you hear at Mass? Explain.

3. What are some ways you can recognize Jesus in the other people you break bread with at Sunday Mass?

4. How can you make your encounter with Jesus at Mass as uplifting and joyous as the disciples' encounter with him on the road to Emmaus?

Many Prayers in One Prayer

The Lord's Prayer includes three forms of prayer: praise, petition, and promise. Identify the type or types of prayer for each phrase of the Lord's Prayer, and then respond to the directives that follow the prayer.

Type of Phrase

Our Father who art in heaven,   _____

hallowed be thy name.   _____

Thy kingdom come.   _____

Thy will be done on earth, as it is in heaven.   _____

Give us this day our daily bread,   _____

and forgive us our trespasses,   _____

    as we forgive those who trespass against us,   _____

and lead us not into temptation,   _____

but deliver us from evil.   _____

For the kingdom, the power
    and the glory are yours, now and forever.   _____

Amen.   _____

1. Write a personal response to one of the petitions you found in the Lord's Prayer.

2. Write a personal response to one of the praises you found in the Lord's Prayer.

3. Write a personal response to one of the promises you found in the Lord's Prayer.

Your Will Be Done, God

Use the following guide to help you discover God's will for you on a decision you face. Write your responses in your reflection notebook.

1. Think of a decision you must make right now.
   Tell God about this decision.

2. How do you feel about this decision?
   Share these feelings with God.

3. What are some of the pros and cons of your decision?
   Explain these pros and cons to God.

4. How will your decision affect other people?
   Discuss the needs of these people with God.

5. What examples from the life or teachings of Jesus relate to your decision?
   Share your insights with God.

6. What do you think is God's will for you in this decision?
   Let God speak to you through your feelings and thoughts.

7. What decision have you made?
   Ask God to help you follow through on your decision.

Many Breads, One Community

Leader: Please join hands and pray the Lord's Prayer together, stopping after the phrase "Give us this day our daily bread." *[The leader starts praying the Lord's Prayer]*

Reader 1: God of everlasting life, bless these rice cakes, fruit of the harvest of countries in Asia. May the taste of rice remind us of the hard work of those who toil in the fields and work for excellence in other areas. Keep us ever mindful of the Asian people who richly gift our culture with their traditions and heritage. Unite us in prayer with them in the blessing and eating of these rice cakes. *[All share in the eating of the rice cakes]*

Reader 2: Creator of the harvest, bless these tortillas, fruit of Latin America. May the taste of tortilla remind us of those who live close to our own homeland and the many who struggle to rise above poverty. Keep us ever mindful of the people of Latin America who richly gift our culture with their traditions and heritage. Unite us in prayer with them in the blessing and eating of these tortillas. *[All share in the eating of the tortillas]*

Reader 3: God of freedom and justice, bless this pita bread, a gift to us from Africa and the Middle East. May the taste of pita remind us of the struggles for freedom in many of these lands, and of the land from which Jesus came. Keep us ever mindful of the people of Africa and the Middle East who richly gift our culture with their traditions and heritage. Unite us in prayer with them in the blessing and eating of this pita bread. *[All share in the eating of the pita bread]*

Reader 4: Grantor of Wisdom, bless this rye bread, a gift from the countries of Europe. May the rich taste of this bread be a reminder of those who settled our country many years ago. Keep us ever mindful of the people of Europe who richly gift our culture with their traditions and heritage. Unite us in prayer with them in the blessing and eating of this rye bread. *[All share in the eating of the rye bread]*

Reader 5: Sustainer God, from whom comes the abundance of the harvest, bless this wheat bread, fruit of the toil of the American farmer. May the taste of this bread remind us of the struggles of the farmer, of those who are paid too little to bake and package the bread, and of those in our country who cannot afford to buy even bread to eat. Keep us ever mindful of all the people in our midst who richly gift our daily life. Unite us in prayer with them in the blessing and eating of this wheat bread. *[All share in the eating of the wheat bread]*

Reader 6: Then Jesus said to them, "Very truly, I tell you, it was not Moses who gave you the bread from heaven, but it is my Father who gives you the true bread from heaven. For the bread of God is that which comes down from heaven and gives life to the world." They said to him, "Sir, give us this bread always."

Jesus said to them, "I am the bread of life. Whoever comes to me will never be hungry, and whoever believes in me will never be thirsty. But I said to you that you have seen me and yet do not believe. Everything that the Father gives me will come to me, and anyone who comes to me I will never drive away; for I have come down from heaven, not to do my own will, but the will of him who sent me. And this is the will of him who sent me, that I should lose nothing of all that he has given me, but raise it up on the last day. This is indeed the will of my Father, that all who see the Son and believe in him may have eternal life; and I will raise them up on the last day." (John 6:32–40)

Leader: Let's join hands again and continue praying the Lord's Prayer. *[The leader continues, "and forgive us our trespasses . . ."]*

Called by the Spirit

The Spirit is active and working to help us "renew the face of the earth." We are challenged to go forth to make peace, serve one another, act justly, heal the sick, and relieve suffering.

Search the periodicals and other resources in the library or media center at school or in your local public library for examples from around the world of Christians doing the work of the Spirit. Find an example for each of the five categories listed here, and prepare a summary of each example to share in class.

Make Peace

Serve One Another

Act Justly

Heal the Sick

Relieve Suffering

Course Evaluation

Please answer the following questions honestly and legibly. Your comments are appreciated and will help to improve this course.

1. Are you glad you took this course? Please explain.

2. List some of the activities you found most worthwhile and tell why you liked them.

3. Which activities seemed lacking? Please explain.

4. Did you find the large class discussions helpful? the small-group discussions? Why or why not?

5. Did you find the written reflection exercises valuable? Please explain.

6. Of all the prayer experiences you participated in during this course, which one did you find the most meaningful? Why?

7. Which chapter of the student text was most helpful? Why?

8. Which chapter of the student text was least helpful? Why?

9. If you could teach this class to next year's students, how would you change it?